THE ATTLAS PROJECT
VOLUME ONE

SEE THE WORLD
IN A NEW LIGHT

ATTILA LEWIS LENDVAI

FIRST EDITION

Written and designed by Attila Lewis Lendvai

Edited by Taposhi Batabyal

Visit www.booksurge.com to order additional copies.

To my parents, family, and friends—
who show me such patience, wisdom, and love

To every teacher, friend and foe alike—
who grow my patience, wisdom, and love

To all that is seen and unseen—
that guides me to SEE the world in a new light
and share it for the benefit of all

To Christine,
Perfect for Halloween...a scary
window into the mind of
the "mad scientist."

Thanks to Dr. Hugh Munro and Wilfrid Laurier University's MBA program
for giving me the space to SEE how far the rabbit hole goes

Thank you John, Shaniqua, Matt, Meredith, and Lauren at Booksurge
for making the publication of my first book go so smoothly

A very special thank-you to my Editor, Taposhi Batabyal,
for providing timely wordsmithing and words of encouragement;
your commitment and confidence have made all the difference

CONTENTS

CONTENTS

INTRODUCTION

It is all too easy to fall into the cynic's trap of overt negativity when writing a prescription for making the world a better place. It will, of course, be necessary to point out certain shortcomings of human civilization, but my intention is to be constructive and offer a positive outlook. Unlike so many contemporary critics, comedians, or commentators, I will not be serving up an all-out, no-holds-barred rant in *the Attlas Project*. Not only is it commonplace in our culture simply to point out what's wrong, it is functionally useless in my opinion. Pick up a newspaper, a remote control, or a mouse and you can see for yourself what's "wrong" with the world. But consider this: when you go to the doctor is it enough for him or her to give you a diagnosis? Don't you want to know what's behind your symptoms? Do you not also expect some medication or treatment program to cure what ails you, if at all possible? So, in writing this book, my challenge is to stay positive, proactive, and constructive. To aid in this effort, I will be presenting a series of diagrams (think blueprints) that should cut down on the rhetoric and make this more of a show and tell, which I hope you will find both entertaining and enlightening. I begin by making a case for hope and optimism.

The Butterfly Effect, the Causal Nature of the Universe, and the Interconnectivity of All Things

"I refuse to believe that God plays dice with the world."

– Albert Einstein.

The scientific theory that micro disturbances can result in macro consequences via a chain of interconnected interactions on an escalating scale is commonly referred to as the butterfly effect. This is the layman's term for chaos theory—the idea that a Monarch butterfly flapping its wings in a Brazilian rainforest can determine whether Florida is hit with a major hurricane. The word "chaos" as it is used here is a bit of a mismatch, since most people associate chaos with randomness, while chaos theory is the study of predictability in apparently random systems. It is an acceptance by science—in theory at least— of a phenomenon described by an ancient Buddhist tenet as the interconnectivity of all things; that is, that even observably random events are, in fact, intrinsically connected (as is the fate of all things) through a never-ending web of cause and effect relationships. The interconnectivity of all things also reflects the implications of yin and yang, Newton's theorem that for every action there is an equal and opposite reaction, and that an infinite number of causes and effects have led to the present state of the observable universe, including the state of our planet, and even that most recent of global human phenomena, the internet.

Even before hypertext and the worldwide web, linguistics had accepted the interconnectivity of all things and the causal, dependent nature of the world. For example, how meaning is derived through language, how language changes over time, and how language and knowledge are indivisible are all factors of interconnectivity. Consider how commonly used expressions change over time, affect culture, and are affected by culture. The science of discourse itself reveals that all human knowledge is dependent on language—even mathematics, physics, and economics. Language and culture constitute and bind human

INTRODUCTION

understanding of all things—like atoms and cells bind and constitute the things themselves. Language and culture also mobilize or constrain us, depending on the circumstances. To see this phenomenon at work, you need only look to the cultures around the world that place a unique set of rules, regulations, and restrictions on women. It may seem unfathomable to some points of view, but when interviewed, many of the women who live under such "repressive" cultures will often highlight a feeling of freedom and happiness that they attribute to the strict codes of conduct by which they must live. They are at once constrained and mobilized by their culture, as we are all constrained and mobilized to one degree or another by the language and culture in which we find ourselves immersed. When it comes to chaos theory and language, we know it takes only a very small shift in human thinking—expressed through language and culture—to result in major constraints and/or mobilizations on a societal, even global scale.

Chaos theory, Buddhism, and linguistics aside, I do not believe there is any reasonable way to deny the fact that the smallest, most insignificant of shifts can lead directly to change on a global if not cosmic scale. Observe a pebble thrown into a pond. Kinetic energy is transferred between molecules (and collections of molecules, i.e., "pebble" and "pond water") via an infinite number of interactions producing an observable pattern of growing scale. For sceptics who might argue that ripples on a pond is an oversimplification of matters, and such childish explanations have no relevance in the complex world of human beings, I simply direct them to human history. A single mutation in a single bacterium followed by a single insect bite probably led to the Black Death and the decimation of the world's population. A single idea, $E=mc^2$, led to the atomic age, the destruction of Hiroshima and Nagasaki, decades of Cold War life, and has yet to play out its final chapter. Will Einstein's legacy end in disastrous consequences; or, finding itself in the hands of enlightened scientists living in a united world of peace and stability, will it end in our unravelling the mysteries of fusion energy, gravity, time, and space? The actions and interactions of individuals acting on perceived crises and opportunities have over the years resulted in everything from the construction of the Great Pyramid at Giza and the rise of the Roman Empire, to the end of British rule in India and the two Gulf Wars. The butterfly effect and the interconnectivity of all things are undeniable, observable processes at work in the world.

Can one person or group change the world? The sceptics and pessimists will want to argue that this is impossible a thousand times before admitting the truth: it has happened, is happening, and will continue to happen until the end of time. The question is not whether there are micro causes that have macro effects. The real question is what micro opportunities do we seize today that will lead to positive macro effects in the future?

Intention and the Process of Change

That is all well and good. Scientists, historians, and meta-physicists alike can agree on the causal nature of the universe. So the universe undergoes change, and, taking evolution as an example, it occurs gradually from moment to moment, generation to generation, involving an infinite number of interactions. So what? What's the significance? All we've accomplished so far is to describe our observations of the process. There must be something more to it, mustn't there? Sure, Marshall McLuhan said "the medium is the message," suggesting the proof is not so much in the pudding, as it is the pudding itself. Does that mean the process has no meaning other than itself? What about intention? Generally speaking, you don't just open your mouth and activate your vocal cords only to let chaos theory run amuck. You intend to say something: express an idea, ask a question, make a command, or any other number of vocalizations by which you intend to express something. The process by which your intention is sent out into the world and received by others is governed by cause and effect— meaning is created through an infinite number of interactions leading up to that moment, including everything from the cultural heritage of the people listening to the nature of speech (the medium) itself. In the world of thought, however, an idea can pretty much just pop into your head without any cause (or apparent relevance)—a non sequitur. In fact, when you observe the constant chatter taking place in your mind, you'll notice that most thought falls into this category. Regardless of how a thought happens to come to you (randomly, a careful thought-process, etc.), or by what method you choose to share it (words, images, music, etc.) the point is that there is an intention to share what's on your mind, or not. This is not the same as claiming you define or control a thought's meaning, it is simply acknowledging some purpose behind the process of thought itself that both supersedes it and is dependent on it.

The debate over intelligent design and evolution is a curious one. This is not the time or place to open the debate—look to volume two of *the Attlas Project* for that proverbial can of worms. For the sake of argument, let's assume for now that natural processes of change—including evolution—are completely random and totally free of intention; i.e. there is no "intelligence" or "higher consciousness" at work. If we make such a claim (provisionally or not) for the process of change in nature, where do we stand on change processes in human phenomenon? For instance, what do we mean by "change management" in business?

Perhaps the best way to approach this question is to examine how humans meddle with natural processes in distinctly intentional (if not entirely "intelligent") ways. For centuries human beings have been actively breeding plants and animals. While our understanding of the process was pretty rudimentary at first, it nonetheless proved effective enough to allow us to breed for certain desirable traits. Later, the detailed study of genetics allowed us to wield even greater power and control over the otherwise "random" natural evolutionary process. We intend to improve our lives with "more perfect" dogs, for instance, or greater crop yields, and fewer genetic diseases, and we express that intention through direct intervention in (and even outright manipulation of) the mechanisms of evolution. We cannot, as of yet, simply snap our fingers and manifest "the ideal" animal, crop, etc. We can, however, have the intention to produce one; and, by understanding the relevant causes and effects, we can make minor genetic adjustments from one generation to the next producing an organism that resembles what we intended, more or less. This kind of genetic manipulation raises serious ethical questions, not least because its application to humanity led to the horrors of eugenics. Nevertheless, the fact remains that human beings possess not only the capability but also the compunction to meddle with nature at its most fundamental levels.

Of course, nature has another way of effecting change on a massive scale which is much more immediate; you could even say violent. Earthquakes, volcanoes, hurricanes, tsunamis, tornadoes...all smack of mass destruction in a matter of moments, with a force of energy well beyond that of any human capacity—not for lack of trying, mind you. Witness clear-cut logging or open-pit mining operations in action with heavy machinery and explosives. It becomes vividly clear that we humans have violent change processes of our own, albeit even our most powerful technologies of destruction—nuclear weapons—pale in comparison with the sheer magnitude of violent forces found in nature. Still, the phenomenon of rapid change on a massive scale is no less a product of cause and effect than the slow methodical pace we observe in evolution. Remember, change is simply a matter of generations of interactions over some time scale; the number, frequency, and kinds of interactions determine the end result. Watch storms on Jupiter through a telescope or compare the surface of the sun to a pot of bubbling fondue: there are shapes and patterns that repeat throughout the universe, all take form and undergo change by virtue of the same process of cause and effect. Any changes we intend to make to natural systems require us to understand, predict, and then act on this fundamental principle.

Change and Humankind

Clearly, human beings participate in natural processes of change. We can be the cause of change in the natural world just as we can see and feel the effects of change come about by so-called random and natural causes. The apparent difference between the two is the fact that we humans can have an intention to create change, defined by some image or definition of what we intend to produce. We cause things to happen that have effects which we hope will produce the intended results. Of course, there are countless examples of unintentional change caused by short-sightedness and unenlightened actions— everything from the decimation of domestic species by the introduction of foreign competitors, to global warming. Either way, people actively participate in the evolutionary process. How, exactly? Let's look at one example out of a near-infinite number of permutations and combinations of cause and effect change processes.

An Example of Intention at Work in a Cause and Effect Change Process

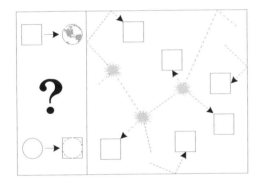

1. Define the Crisis and/or *Opportunity*. A square peg won't "work" given a round hole; so an entrenched system of square pegs, evolved over many generations (and acting / interacting accordingly), certainly won't "work" in a world that is defined by round holes. Luckily, every square has an inherent *potential for roundness* inside.

2. Create and Communicate an *Intention*. Formulate and introduce (envision and inspire; design and install) *the intention for roundness* into the established system of square pegs.

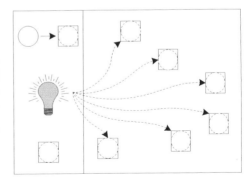

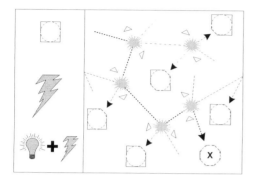

3. Act (and Interact) with Intention.
The system, with the intention of roundness installed, functions as usual producing small incremental changes to participants with every action / interaction. The change process is accelerated by proactive participants focused on *their intention*—and *their potential*—for roundness (**X**).

4. Wait and Watch the *Transformation*.
Many generations of intentional actions and interactions, each having just a small incremental effect on participants, will over time produce the intended transformation: first, on an individual basis (**X**), then system wide. The result is a system of square pegs evolved to "work" in a world full of round holes.

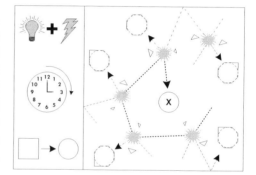

So what about human phenomena—human systems—like economics, governance, and culture? Although the structures of modern civilization seem monolithic, ingrained, purely intentional, and resilient to change, they are in fact emergent systems that have evolved throughout history. And, just like in the natural world, evolved human systems that do not exhibit the traits necessary to survive ever-changing circumstances (or those that cannot adapt quickly enough) tend to go extinct. The diagrams above show how we can install a new intention (idea, design, etc.) into an established system and allow it to chip away at the so-called monolithic structure over time until it is transformed—evolved and improved. As suggested, the key is instilling and installing an enlightened intention into all elements of the established system. This means creating and communicating an actionable solution simply, efficiently, and effectively. It is especially important to plant the seeds of change or "turn the wheel on the

Titanic a few degrees" sooner rather than later, especially if there is a risk that the system faces extinction. If we act too late, there are other approaches to change in the universe—already discussed—that are far more immediate, decisive, and ultimately destructive. As a species, our choices right now are: change or die or change by dying; but make no mistake: change is coming sooner or later, one way or the other.

Following the logic outlined in this section, what is needed is to define the crises/opportunities; create and communicate the intentions; act and interact on those intentions (with only small impacts on participants); and watch and wait for the natural transformation process to do its thing.

Enter *the Attlas Project*

This is the start of a life's work. When it comes to people, you can often trace their purpose in life back to childhood. We often hear it said that Mozart was born to be a great composer, Gandhi was destined to show the world a new way to win India's freedom, Michael Phelps was made for swimming, etc. In my life I've observed that most people simply walk the earth (and there's nothing wrong with that!), some appear born to tread on it (which can be problematic when they tread on others), and still others seem destined to support it and raise it higher. At the risk of sounding egotistical, I've always counted myself among the latter group, along with the untold numbers of individuals who spend time daily helping others or using their talents and gifts for the betterment of humankind and the planet.

Ever since I was a child I've had an insatiable appetite for knowledge, a knack for deconstructing phenomena, an ability to recognize the shapes and patterns that make them work (or not), and a passion for revealing ways to make them better. As I grew older the phenomena expanded and my passion to deconstruct and discuss them intensified, and, since natural phenomena tend to work just fine, my attention turned to the big picture of humanity—warts and all. Having a passion for deconstructing the world, engaging others, and exchanging ideas for making the world a better place was one thing; doing so in a way that resulted in something other than an allergic reaction was another matter entirely! I came to realize that miscommunication, misinterpretation, and misunderstanding formed a dense fog of scepticism, distrust, even fear among most people; and, this fog kept them from ever stepping outside of the comfort and safety of their entrenched worldviews. I saw a fundamental disconnect between human behaviour and the necessary conditions for making the world a better place—the free flow of enlightened, shareable, doable ideas among individuals. Overcoming this hurdle was step one in my life's work (and is Chapter one of this book). SEE VISUAL AID (Strategize, Engage, and Execute via Virtual Interactive Simulation, Universal Adaptive Language, and Actionable Intelligence Discourse) grew out of a necessity to overcome the inherent weaknesses of language as a way of thinking, sharing, and doing; it became my primary operating system for analyzing needs/opportunities; creating and communicating solutions; and executing action plans. I came to know my purpose as show, don't tell; and, as the old saying goes, the show must go on.

After nearly two decades since high school following my life's work down several different paths, from theatre and film, to teaching, to business consulting, I have come full circle to the place where I first began to see who I really am and what I have to give: a simple process for deconstructing the world, recognizing shapes and patterns that make it work (or not), creating ways to make it better, and sharing solutions that are completely and utterly doable. This book is the result of years of that work: a handful of easy-to-follow blueprints for upgrading the world of humankind—a set of micro opportunities that, if seized today, will have positive macro effects in the future.

On the question of ego, I'll address that issue in more detail in Volume two. For now, the observant should note that when you take the "I" out of Attila's you're left with Attlas. In all humility, the purpose of *the Attlas Project* is to show; and, the show must go on. So, without further ado, it's time to...

SEE THE WORLD IN A NEW LIGHT

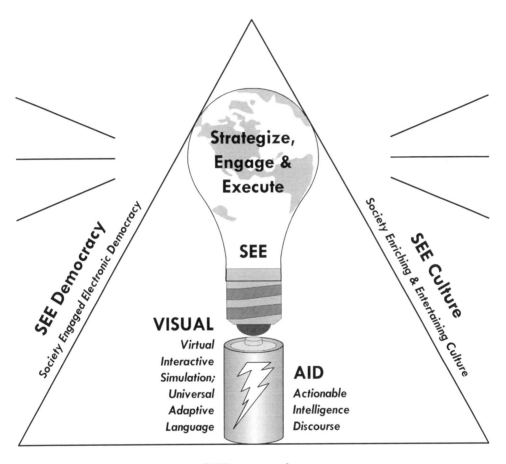

Strategize, Engage & Execute

SEE

SEE Democracy
Society Engaged Electronic Democracy

SEE Culture
Society Enriching & Entertaining Culture

VISUAL
Virtual
Interactive
Simulation;
Universal
Adaptive
Language

AID
Actionable
Intelligence
Discourse

SEEconomics
Social & Environmental Economics

THE ATTLAS PROJECT

VOLUME ONE

SEE VISUAL AID

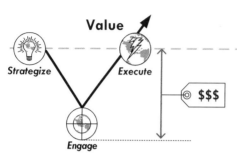

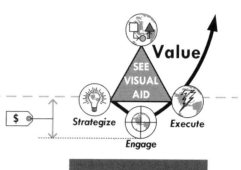

MAXIMUM VALUE

Strategize	**E**ngage	**E**xecute
V I S	U A L	A I D

Virtual / Interactive / Simulation / Universal / Adaptive / Language / Actionable / Intelligence / Discourse

The Value of SEE VISUAL AID Just Adds Up:

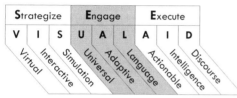

Strategize with Virtual Interactive Simulation

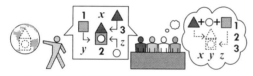

Engage with Universal Adaptive Language

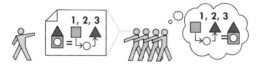

Execute with Actionable Intelligence Discourse

SEE, Show, Tell & Sell Efficiently, Effectively, Exactly

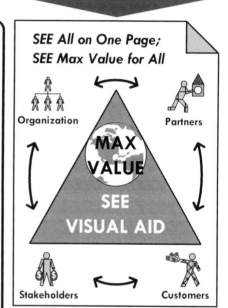

SEE All on One Page;
SEE Max Value for All

Organization — Partners

MAX VALUE — SEE VISUAL AID

Stakeholders — Customers

ALL ON ONE PAGE

Organization — 1, 2, 3 — Partners

Stakeholders — Customers

CHAPTER ONE
SEE VISUAL AID

A Question of Value

Value

Strategize   *Execute*

Does strategy have any value without execution? To put it another way, does a plan, idea, or even a thought pertaining to the real world serve any practical purpose if it cannot be applied? You probably have hundreds, if not thousands, of thoughts each day which, at best, simply lead to other thoughts; dozens of ideas and even a few plans that end up going nowhere and producing nothing more than other ideas and plans. We will get into the nature, structure, and function of thinking later. For now, let's assume that the intention of thinking about the world is that the thoughts, ideas, and plans we make are realized, applied, or executed—somehow, somewhere, sometime—and if they are not, then they have no purpose, practically speaking. Unfulfilled intentions are certainly not on many people's list of things to strive for. So by applying a little common sense, we can safely say that strategy has little or no value without execution.

Creating Value

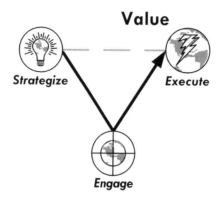

Can a strategy be executed without engagement? Think about it carefully: is a plan, idea, or thought pertaining to the real world doable without at least some interaction of some kind with that world? Engaging at least one other person or one other element in the world is a prerequisite to executing any strategy. To help simplify things, let's look at communication as one form of engagement: an act of engaging others.

A typical definition of the word communication is the act of conveying information, but this definition deserves some unpacking. For starters, the word "conveying" is itself a loaded term. From where is the information being conveyed? To whom or where is it being conveyed? We sometimes forget that communication is a two-way street. We receive information just as readily as we give it—both are acts of conveying—and this giving and receiving of information happens, not a couple of hundred or a few thousand times, but millions of times per day. At first glance, this is a surprise. If you are sitting alone in a comfortable chair with no one around to talk to, for example, you may be wondering how, exactly, you are communicating. For starters, you are reading this book, so you are receiving information. But even if you were not reading, even if you were sitting alone in a pitch-black room, your mind would constantly be chattering. Not only that, your brain would never stop sending signals throughout your body and getting signals back, whether internal or external in nature. The very act of processing information, even if only in your mind, entails communication. From one moment to the next, so long as your mind and body are alive, doing practically anything requires communication—conveying information from one place to another.

We need to look at communication not so much as an act of engaging but as a state of being engaged. To be alive is to be in a state of communication at all times with internal and external environments. Another term for this is mediation. Since all sensory inputs, all thoughts pertaining to those inputs, all outputs, and all thoughts pertaining to those outputs are processed in the brain, all knowledge is mediated. But this is only the beginning. The brain processes different kinds of inputs and outputs (namely sight, sound, touch, taste, and smell). Since this is the case, our whole understanding of the world exists in one medium or another or a combination—a form of multimedia. In order to engage the world, we mediate external inputs and internal thought processes to produce strategies that are further mediated via outputs in order to execute these same strategies. But even this is too superficial an analysis of what it means to be in a state of mediation.

How do we mediate? By what processes and using what technology? Consider for a moment how we think. For the most part, we think in shapes and patterns. We think in languages. We see things in the world and we visualize images in our minds. We hear music in the real world and in our heads. We listen to speeches given to us in life and we rehearse speeches we are planning to give ahead of time. We engage the three-dimensional world by getting our hands dirty: touching, experimenting, trying to fit part "A" into slot "B," arranging, re-arranging, taking things apart, and putting them back together again (without, we hope, too many "mystery parts" left over!). We do this in our minds, too. The point is, when it comes to engaging the world, our intention is to make the act of mediation as accurate and true to life as possible. This ensures our understanding of the world is of a high quality, our strategies to tackle situations are more likely to work, and the execution of these strategies will be as accurate and true to our intentions as possible. As the old cliché goes, nothing in life worth having comes without a price; so it goes for being in a state of engagement.

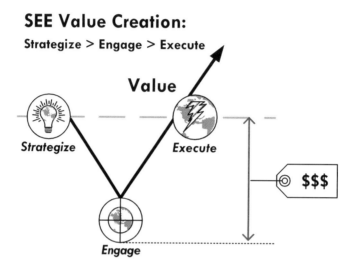

SEE Value Creation:
Strategize > Engage > Execute

In order to create value in the SEE process (Strategy, Engagement, Execution), it follows that some investment must be made. That investment is engagement: the bridge between strategy and execution. The greater the distance between strategy and execution, the greater the investment of time, effort, frustration, etc. made in the engagement process. This doesn't need much elaboration: we all know how miscommunication, misinterpretation, and misunderstanding can bring the best-laid plans to a standstill. Recall the classic Abbott and Costello baseball sketch, "Who's on First?" (a comedy routine that defies all attempts at verbal description; I highly recommend looking it up online if you are unfamiliar with it or cannot recall it). What may not be apparent is that this distance—between strategy and execution—is not set in stone. It is directly dependent on the quality of the engagement process; for instance, the efficiency and efficacy of the communication between individuals involved in the process. By employing a more powerful communication methodology, you make the engagement process more efficient and effective (you reduce the distance in time and space between thinking and doing) thus reducing the costs associated with executing the strategy.

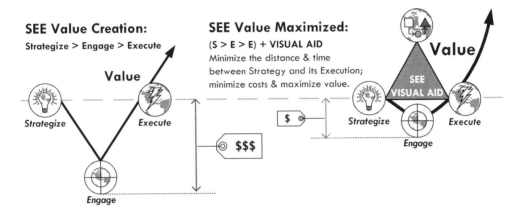

Moreover, communication (which is more accurately understood as mediation) includes listening (awareness, analysis, synthesis, and understanding). A more effective mediation methodology increases the likelihood that:

1. **Strategic analysis of real-world needs is sound in the first place.**
2. **Engagement process is true to the intentions of the strategy.**
3. **Execution of strategy more effectively meets real-world needs.**

Knowledge is Power

This well-worn cliché needs little explanation or elaboration. It is enough to say that knowledge is a prerequisite to strategy and that communication (mediation) is the path to creation and execution of strategy. Media and language (the basis of mediation and communication) must also be the basis of knowledge itself. Let's explore this concept and its implications in the context of power in more detail.

Knowledge as Media

Think about it for a moment: we know things in our mind. No matter how you slice it, any "thing" processed in our mind is a representation of the thing we are thinking about, and not the thing itself. Sharing knowledge (via language, visuals, multimedia presentations, etc.) is not only a representation, it is also a re-presentation—a mediated presentation of what started out as only a representation in our mind. The resulting knowledge in the mind of the recipient (reader, observer, etc.), is likewise another representation of the thing that was presented to them in some mediated form (a re-presented representation of the original). Recall, if you will, the "broken telephone" game you may have played as a child, or the gossip which may or may not occur in your office, extended family, or circle of friends. The point is this: after multiple retellings, it is rare for the original facts of the story to remain intact. Another way to think about this phenomenon is to consider making a photocopy of a photocopy of a photograph. No matter how powerful the photocopier you are using, it is inevitable that the resolution and quality of the image will be reduced with each reproduction. In the case of language as the intermediary, each and every transfer of knowledge is open to interpretation (and therefore misinterpretation and misunderstanding).

Knowledge as Language

Countless critics, philosophers, scientists, and psychologists have studied language throughout the years and it is not my intention to provide a survey of all their discoveries and/or theories. For the purposes of this book, I will summarize language as being an operating system for civilization built on a complex code: a mediation of the world, whose primary role is to enable a shared understanding of that world between humans. Again, for practical purposes, I will refrain from exploring language in the animal kingdom, recognizing that the gamut of communication and shared understanding among creatures runs far, wide, and well beyond the limited scope of human experience and understanding—from hive mentality to whale society. For human beings at least, language has been the dominant modus operandi by which we have arrived at our understanding of the universe and our place in it; this understanding forms the foundation of human society, culture, and civilization—science, faith, law, et al. I do not seek to deconstruct the nature and inner workings of language, nor is it my intention to criticize the limitations of language as if I am advocating its abolishment. I could never propose abandoning the operating system that mediated everyone from great spiritual teachers and Shakespeare to great political leaders and lyricists. Without it, we would be hard pressed to formulate and share our thoughts, particularly those of an abstract nature. That said, the fact that language has become the fundamental operating system of society, culture, and civilization is problematic. I cannot responsibly propose an upgrade to such an operating system without pointing out some of its inherent deficiencies and—dare I say—flaws.

The Power of Visualization

Without question, the most valuable form of mediation human beings have is visualization. We use visual aids to accomplish everything from building houses to driving cars. Nothing is more ubiquitous and universal, for instance, than the arrow. An arrow points us in a direction or points out something of potential interest. It does so thanks to shared human history dating back tens of thousands of years (from hunter-gatherers to trader-travellers to ruler-warriors), during which the bow and arrow (and later the compass needle) was an essential survival tool to literally hit the target and/or stay on course. Naturally it would evolve into a universally accepted and understood symbol. Likewise the square, circle, triangle, and myriad other shapes and patterns can readily be understood by peoples around the world. From the simplest drawing to the most advanced schematic diagram, human beings tend to "get it" when "it" approximates, enhances, exaggerates, simplifies, focuses, or otherwise visually represents the real world. A few clichés come to mind here: seeing is believing, and a picture is worth a thousand words.

One of the reasons visual aids are so powerful is that they often convey actionable intelligence; that is, the information you need to know at the moment you need to know it to take action. Highway road signs are an example. There's not much use in knowing if your lane ends fifty kilometres down the highway. It is important, however, to know if your lane ends in one kilometre, 500 metres, or right now! A football team needs to know its plays by heart (think of the typical chalkboard drawings of X's and O's) so that at the moment the quarterback calls the play, all the players are literally on the same page, as well as being on the same field. Surveyors, foremen, builders, and tradespeople turn to blueprints when constructing a building to give them the precise information they need in order to coordinate their work.

Now ask yourself this: if visual aids work for engineers, architects, software designers, drivers, football teams, military strategists, and in a host of other real-world applications, why not for high level strategy (i.e., business, non-profit, government)? How often have you sat in meetings that have been talk-fests, at best? Hours go by and little, if anything, gets accomplished. There is nothing to show for the investment of time and effort. Have you watched a session of Parliament (or Congress) lately? It seems the whole exercise is just for show, with little or nothing to show for it. What about reading a lengthy legal document or government report? It seems that the sheer mass of written material is supposed to show how much time, thought, and effort went into it, but at times it is all but impossible to extract any real actionable intelligence. What about an instruction manual that has few, if any, illustrations or diagrams? Think of a few more examples from your own experience that illustrate the fact that communication (mediation, engagement) between human beings is at times the weakest precisely when it needs to be the strongest—that is, when we need to actually get things done in the real world.

SEE VISUAL AID – The Power to get Things done in the World

The solution to getting things done more efficiently, effectively, exactly, and with the least number of headaches is to SEE VISUAL AID at work. The following chart breaks down each component and its application in the SEE process.

Strategize	Engage	Execute
V	I	S	U	A	L	A	I	D

Virtual Interactive Simulation Universal Adaptive Language Actionable Intelligence Discourse

The purpose of breaking down the concept of using visual aids in this way is to illustrate the depth of meaning, purpose, and power of visualization in each of the component parts of the SEE process: thinking, showing, and doing. For instance, the priority function of visualization during the strategic planning phase is Virtual Interactive Simulation, while the priority function during the execution process is Actionable Intelligence Discourse. And yet it should be made clear that the substance of any simulation during the strategy process carries over into the other processes. To illustrate this point better, let us walk through all three phases and visualize the continuity and distinctiveness of SEE VISUAL AID throughout the process.

Strategize with Virtual Interactive Simulation

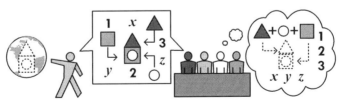

Strategize with Virtual Interactive Simulation

The strategy phase begins first and foremost with observation—recognizing shapes and patterns in the relevant circumstances pertaining to the real-world challenge being faced. In classical problem-solving, we would call this defining the problem: identifying the variables, parameters, and limits that apply given a certain set of circumstances. Once a real-world situation has been broken down into component parts, analysis of how these parts interact with and affect the whole can take place (i.e., defining the key variables affecting the outcome). In the case of a mechanic tearing down an engine, for instance, this process is hands-on. But in the case of an automobile designer, being hands-on is not that simple. It is costly and time-consuming to even make models of preliminary designs, let alone full-blown prototypes. So, early sketches and concept drafts are shown to engineers before models (computerized and/or scale) are made for wind tunnel tests and the like. This is virtual interactive simulation: approximating real-world conditions to test theories, approaches, and strategies for solving problems in a more efficient manner than real-world trial and error, but just as effective. Identifying shapes and patterns, interacting with others, and being hands-on are best practices in the strategizing process (thinking, problem solving).

Of course, it is not always possible to be hands-on in the strictest sense. Consider the management team of a multinational corporation or the head of a government agency approaching the design of a strategic program or redesign of an existing department. There is no way to interact physically with the object of the strategy, yet hands-on interaction among the team is still essential: therefore, Virtual Interactive Simulation is essential. Does a talk-fest suffice? Or does adhering to generic models of strategy (such as the Diamond-E) actually do justice to the task at hand? 3M is one company who understands the power of visualization as a tool for Virtual Interactive Simulation. They have made "white boarding" a standard practice in most boardrooms; and now, they even have electronic white boards capable of digitizing drawings for practical distribution and use beyond the meeting. White boarding sessions still involve a good deal of talking—explanation, elaboration, contextualization, argumentation, etc.—but participants stay focused on the white board and the emerging visual aid. This is how people connect with a collective understanding of a problem and collaborate on a possible solution.

Whether they are working in a group or on an individual basis, highly effective people choose from countless visualization strategies to approach Virtual Interactive Simulation. I am sure you're familiar with brainstorming or "the brain dump." This is where you take a blank sheet of paper, put the subject/topic in the centre and proceed to write down (in single words or short phrases) anything and everything you can think of relating to that topic. The result of a brainstorming session, especially one that has been well-facilitated, is a mind map—a big picture overview of everything in your head related and/or relevant to the topic at hand. In fact, more sophisticated versions of brainstorming are actually called mind mapping exercises. While there are likely many formal schools of thought on what mind maps should look like, I have never been keen on limiting the process. In classical eras, there was a certain look or style paintings needed to have. Were it not for the pioneering visionaries who broke free from the formalism of their day, we might never have seen the wonders of impressionism and modernism in art. It is important to realize that, in the strategizing phase, the more formalized the Virtual Interactive Simulation process, the more limited your creativity. This is the case because brainstorming, mind-mapping, whatever you call it—call it thinking on paper—is just that: thinking.

There is a common misconception that human beings are capable of unmediated thought. Some believe that mediation only comes into play when we try to communicate our thoughts. As we've already seen, mediation is not an act; it is a state of being. All our thoughts are already mediated. Yet it is important to note that there is nothing absolute or pure about visualization. The brain must still piece images together from somewhere and project them on the internal canvas of the mind's eye. The question is: how many of us have such a robust internal canvas that we can fully articulate a complete strategy in our minds, zoom in on specific elements, make changes to these elements if necessary, and then zoom back out and see how those changes affect the overall big picture? Exactly: very few people have that capacity. So we use brainstorming, mind mapping, flow-charting, and a myriad other visual tools and techniques to help us think. There is no fundamental difference between the internal and external thought/visualization processes during any strategy session—both are mediated representations of actions and events affecting real-world outcomes. The differences lay in the relative strengths and weaknesses of each.

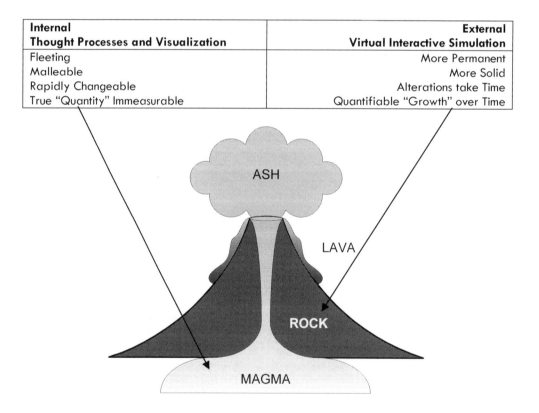

Internal **Thought Processes and Visualization**	External **Virtual Interactive Simulation**
Fleeting	More Permanent
Malleable	More Solid
Rapidly Changeable	Alterations take Time
True "Quantity" Immeasurable	Quantifiable "Growth" over Time

We can think of internal thought and visualization as the crucible of a volcano, hot magma bubbling upwards and flowing outwards, quite malleable and impermanent. External thought and visualization, on the other hand, is what happens to magma when it reaches the surface (for starters, we now call it lava) and cools—it slows, hardens into more solid shapes and patterns, and becomes more permanent (eventually set in stone). A volcano, like thought, exists as both internal and external processes simultaneously. The external accumulation of volcanic rock is what grows the volcano, just as our understanding of a particular topic grows as we get it down on paper. In the analogy, ash represents the knowledge by-products of the eruption of internal and external thought. Anyone who has ever gone through any kind of brainstorming process knows how much of it ends up on the cutting room floor, as it were. The power of this analogy is in its simplicity and real-world truth: just as terra-forming is dependent to an enormous degree on volcanic activity (hot magma from within the earth coming to the surface and being exposed to the elements without), so too is our worldview dependent on internal thoughts being externalized and documented in multimedia formats. We cannot truly think about the world without some kind of concrete interaction and simulation. We cannot grow, develop, or share our knowledge of the world without some form of visualization or documentation (mediation of some kind): think of a volcano in action; Strategize with Virtual Interactive Simulation.

Engage with Universal Adaptive Language

Engage with Universal Adaptive Language

We've already established that strategy has little or no practical value unless it can be executed, and that the process of acting on an idea requires engaging the world—meaning other people—in a practical, meaningful way. Whether it is the genius inventor tucked away in a basement somewhere who secretly discovers a pollution-free technology to solve the world's energy problems or the ascetic who achieves enlightenment atop a solitary mountain retreat, personal achievement—as remarkable and admirable as it may be—has little practical value from humanity's perspective unless it makes a positive contribution to a shared human experience. Therefore the genius likely patents and licenses his invention for use by governments and large corporations. The ascetic comes down from the mountain and counsels leaders, lawmakers, artists, and society as a whole from an enlightened perspective. In either case, the method used to engage the world has a direct impact on the shared value created. What value is created, how much, when, and for whom?

It is not by accident that human beings have developed so many different methods of engaging one another. We are compelled to do so. From the simplest sounds and symbols to the most sophisticated languages, it's all about engagement: that state of oneness that connects two or more beings intellectually and/or emotionally. Who among us has not felt the urge to share the latest tidbit of juicy gossip, let alone some revelation or discovery that has been a lifetime in the making? The drive to share our thoughts and feelings with others is the tenacious impulse behind a myriad variety of human interactions. Now consider this: when compelled to share an idea, do you settle on a method of engaging others that is ill-suited to the task? How do you choose your method of interaction? Or, is this choice made unconsciously; do you simply fall back on some default method of engaging others, whether it is ideally suited to your needs or not?

It is often said of Mozart that complete scores presented themselves to him in his mind's eye (or rather, his mind's ear). Clearly, he was compelled to share his revelations and did so using the methodology he knew best: playing and writing music. Mozart was trained relentlessly from a very young age in the art of music, and so hearing, playing, and writing down musical notes—the language of music—seemed to come naturally to him. Have you ever asked the question of which came first in Mozart's case: the inspiration or the talent? What if he had been trained from an early age instead to be a great chocolatier? Would complete concertos and symphonies still have presented themselves to him? More to the point, what would he have done with such musical inspiration, had he been trained in the mastery of chocolate instead of music? On the one hand this line of questioning is purely hypothetical, but on the other, it is an entirely relevant and down-to-earth question to ask in the context of human engagement. It highlights a situation to which just about everyone can relate at some point in their life.

Have you ever found yourself at a loss for words? You know the feeling: when you just cannot seem to adequately express yourself. It's the kind of situation that gets our inner voice saying things like: "If only I had read more books as a child..." or "if only I had paid more attention in Ms. Pettigrew's grade 11 English class." I'm sure we have all felt like that at one point or another in our lives. In our globalized world, we've likely encountered people who don't speak our language and know how challenging and frustrating it can be trying to interact with someone who you cannot understand and who cannot understand you. But this phenomenon does not only apply to language. What about those times when what you need to communicate successfully is a picture? You can see it in your mind's eye, but don't have the drawing skills to reproduce it, and must rely on a verbal description in an attempt to try to get the other person to "see" what the heck it is you're talking about. Even a mastery of the English language cannot adequately convey the value of hearing a Mozart symphony, examining a schematic diagram, or viewing the Mona Lisa. Very few of us consider ourselves enough of an artist, musician, writer, speaker, designer, engineer, scientist, architect and so forth to successfully create a shared experience from our thoughts using the method of engagement (language) most appropriate to it. And what about those ideas that do not fall neatly into an established discipline equipped with its own language? In either case, when we are compelled to share an idea beyond the limits of our communication skills, we have no choice but to fall back on whatever language (and level of mastery) we are familiar with. Herein lies the plight and the paradox of humanity since the dawn of civilization: when it comes to many of the ideas we consider potentially most valuable, we are literally at a loss for words.

All methods of communication strive to meet certain practical needs relating to human interaction and have evolved organically over time according to those needs. As human experience grows in scale, scope, and complexity, our methods of engaging and sharing that experience with one another evolves accordingly (including wisdom, science, arts, history, law, economics, and the societies based on them). This growth applies to all information, communication, and imaging systems: compare the cave drawings of our ancestors to the works of renaissance masters and modern photo-realistic images, not to mention digital photography, computer-aided design (CAD), and virtual reality simulation. Consider that once upon a time if physicians wanted to see inside the body, they had to reach for a knife. Thank goodness doctors agreed they needed a less invasive way of seeing inside patients, and began using non-invasive physical examinations with medical illustrations; later, they added x-ray, ultrasound, fibre optics, magnetic resonance, and other imaging technologies. No one method replaced all the previous ones; rather, they worked in tandem to flesh out the medical profession's ability to engage patients visually. That said, all these methods of engaging patients have greatly reduced—if not entirely eliminated— the need for invasive surgery. So, as medicine grew in scale, scope and complexity, medical imaging—as an integral part of the way doctors engage patients and share information—followed suit.

While this is fine for languages related to areas of specialized knowledge like medicine or engineering, what about language in general? We probably have more living languages in the world today than in any other time in our history. Certainly in terms of sheer numbers, we have more people speaking different languages now than in any other time in our history, and more of those people are engaging each other at home and abroad, thanks to relatively easy access to rapid travel, telecommunications, mass media, and of course the internet. And, while English has spread all over the globe (after several centuries of use by two superpowers—colonial England and post-colonial United States), this only complicates matters. English is a hodgepodge that continues to assimilate words, syntax, expressions, and idioms from around the globe, making it difficult to learn and even more difficult to master. I have personal experience teaching English as a second language and know all too well the trials faced by those struggling to cope with exceptions to every rule, let alone trying to make heads or tails of "the latest buzz on the street" lest they get "tagged by the man" or worse, some "big kahuna pops a cap in their ass." Sound melodramatic? Tell that to Polish immigrant Robert Dziekanski who, unable to communicate in English and scared because he couldn't find his mother, died in Vancouver International Airport on October 14, 2007 after police jolted him with a taser. You read that right—not Afghanistan, not Darfur, not even Guantanamo Bay, Cuba, but Vancouver, Canada. I'm sure you'll agree there is something very wrong with someone dying due to language, generally speaking (pun very much intended).

The world is in many ways a very different place than it was one thousand, one hundred, or even ten years ago. I don't think anyone can reasonably deny the challenges facing humanity as a whole are greater in number, scale, scope, and complexity than ever before. The trouble is that humanity has yet to recognize a single, simple, universally applicable language with which to engage, understand, and share all the challenges it faces—let alone strategize, engage, and execute potential solutions. Not for lack of trying: most empires arose with one dominant language which played a major role in the subjugation of and domination over other nations, cultures, and peoples. Thankfully, gone are the days of a single language being forced upon the subjects of a massive dominant empire (i.e., Latin). Picking a single existing language and imposing it on the rest of the world has never worked nor will it. There is too much baggage bundled up with the language of any given society: its history, nationality, culture, art, religion...passion. As a written and spoken legacy of a particular human experience, how can any language claim sovereignty over the whole of human experience—past, present, and future?

We have seen the proliferation of western capitalism, law, democracy, culture, food, fashion, and industry throughout the world in direct parallel to the spread of the English language, the language spoken by the United States and by at least one nation on almost every continent. And yet, despite all this, English has not—and will not—achieve status as the planet's universal language. For starters, English is by any measure inefficient, ineffective, and down-right difficult to use let alone master. As mentioned earlier, its roots and history have given it a character that is altogether chaotic: grammatically, idiosyncratically, and culturally. No matter what English-speaking country you visit in the world, you will encounter a different version of the language. With its proliferation and application across countless sectors of society and culture, it has amassed an enormous lexicon. The rampant use of the internet and cell phones among young people has further affected the language for future generations, where expressions like "LOL" and "Talk 2 U L8r" are turning up in high school essays almost as frequently as in chat rooms and text messages. But let's back up a second: it's entirely unfair to lay blame on the masses for a language's so-called degradation. If anything, the people represent the living language—ever-evolving real-world experiences reflected in their system for understanding and sharing them. What about the courts, where adults argue in public the letter of the law and the spirit of the law? If laws written in English are open to interpretation—supplemented by hundreds if not thousands of pages of legal precedents—then what's the point of trying to establish it as the de facto universal language? Perhaps if Hollywood one day achieves its goals of world cultural domination, English may succeed in infecting every society around the globe; but that will in no way fix its deficiencies as an operating system to enable a near-digital-quality shared experience among human beings.

There are other methods of human engagement vying for the position of dominant language. First, there's economics (and commerce). Economics is a language as any other, a way for human beings to understand the world and one another.   Commerce is a particular kind of interaction—identification, agreement, and exchange of material value. Science, too, makes a strong bid for the spot of universal language: a standard set of methods for the study and exchange of knowledge relating to the natural world. One quickly realizes, however, that numbers (mathematics) are an integral part of the foundations of both economics and science, not to mention technology, geometry, music, visual art, and more. Surely numbers and the rules of mathematics are universally accepted the world over. Numbers are of course the best system we have to communicate certain kinds of information (exact quantitative data), but they are simply not up to the task of conveying qualitative data. And let us not forget that linguistics still play an integral role in both economics and science, so despite the universal acceptance and use of tools like the periodic table of the elements, scientific and economic engagement still requires a good deal of translation (even translations of numbers themselves: think of the variability of currency exchange rates from one day to the next around the world).

Is there an answer, then? Does the potential even exist for a universal adaptive language that enables human beings to efficiently and effectively engage one another and the world in which they live? The answer, boldly stated, is yes.

The key is not to fall into the trap of isolation and protectionism that define all other languages. Since all languages developed over time with specific real-world needs in mind, they tended to focus on the aspect of the world they intended to engage (i.e., mathematics' focus on quantitative evaluation). But one cannot hope to establish a universally adaptable and acceptable language unless it includes, at least in theory, all languages, methods of communication, traditions, etc. By leaving nothing out, no one and nothing is left out: that means nothing is beyond the scope of its capability, and its use and mastery is beyond the scope of no one. A universally adaptive language has no rules per se; rather, it has intention. That intention is to make a digital connection with any number of other human beings in the most efficient, effective, and intellectually satisfying way possible given the circumstances.

What does a universal adaptive language look like? You've already seen it in action. You've been engaging with it throughout this book. You engage it each and every day of your life, taking for granted the universal adaptive language in which the very universe is written. When did you ever study what the shape of a human being meant? Surely somewhere along the line as a child your experience of human beings caused you to associate a whole series of thoughts and feelings with the human form, some of which may be thought of as positive and some negative. You probably have certain unique associations with the male form, the female form, your own, and that of your mother or father. But these are specific associations based on specific versions of the human form. Strip away that specificity and what you're left with are at least a handful of general, universal associations with the shape of a human being. This is due in no small part to the fact that in general there are certain inalienable experiences common to all human beings: shared experiences. Think back to the beginning of this discussion of engagement and recall that it is the goal of all human engagement to transform an individual experience of a thought or an idea into some form of shared experience. It makes sense, then, to base a universal adaptive language on elements from humanity's shared experience.

All of humankind recognizes shapes and patterns. All of humankind counts and evaluates quantitatively (the integration of numbers and mathematics). All of humanity indicates direction or directs others by pointing, either with a finger or an arrow. Human beings put things inside containers. We all use boxes, cylinders, vessels of every conceivable shape and size. We sort things by category. We label things; both objective (nouns: dog, cat, tree, shrub) and subjective (adjectives: big, small, beautiful, prickly). Every way of knowing, every intellectual tradition, all academic disciplines, the perception of all natural phenomena, even some aspects of our existence that cannot be perceived with any of the five human senses can be represented efficiently, effectively, and exactly with a combination of visual, numerical, geometric, and linguistic elements that are universal to all humankind.

So what about words? If there is no universal written/spoken language, how is it possible to integrate them into a universally adaptive language? The key here is "universally adaptive." When a linguistic label is used in conjunction with a visual form, there is very little chance of miscommunication, misinterpretation, misunderstanding, or mistranslation. The word "human" may be written and pronounced differently in every dialect in the world, and is subject to mistranslation; but the label "human" next to the image of a human being cannot be misunderstood or mistranslated by any reasonable person. In a universal adaptive language, linguistics and visualizations are both kept simple and work together to minimize complexity. The universal adaptive language itself is infinitely adaptive and complex in order to achieve its intention of enabling human beings to create a shared understanding of experience.

Execute with Actionable Intelligence Discourse

Execute with Actionable Intelligence Discourse

We have already established that an idea or thought has little to no practical value unless it can engage the world—other people—in some form. The same can be said for a shared idea or understanding among many people that cannot be applied practically in the world. There have been countless examples of this phenomenon throughout history, including the attempts by organized religion to create a heaven-on-earth scenario for believers. However, since religion is something of a Pandora's Box, I do not wish to open it at this time. Let us consider instead another shared vision of human beings: the dream of flight.

I'm sure that even in ancient times more than one human had the thought, "I want to fly" or "Wouldn't it be great if we human beings could fly?" Now, it shouldn't come as any surprise that these humans probably thought more along the lines of "I want to be able to fly like a bird," because after all, birds flew. It is also not surprising, then, that some of the earliest concepts of flying humanoids—angels—had bird-like wings. In Greek mythology, Icarus flies too close to the sun with a pair of bird-like wings made of wax and Hercules rides Pegasus, the winged horse. Practically speaking, these human and mythological beings believed they were on to something: after all, birds flew with bird-like wings; ergo, for something to fly it also needs bird-like wings. It's very logical. Sadly, it would take hundreds if not thousands of failed and near-fatal attempts at executing this shared idea before a real breakthrough in human flight was achieved. This delay wasn't because the desire to achieve human flight was inherently wrong or unnatural in any way, it was due to the fact that early aviators were acting upon incomplete intelligence. They couldn't see the big picture. From simple aerodynamics to complex bird biomechanics that manipulate airflow and make flight possible—for birds and humans alike—their shared idea, "I want to fly like a bird," was limited by their shared system of engaging the world at the time—their discourse.

Leonardo Da Vinci, the renaissance master painter, thinker, and engineer had a knack for observation. Like many great artists, philosophers, scientists, and other thinkers throughout history, Da Vinci could see things that others missed. His attention to detail was phenomenal, yet in some of his greatest works, that detail is subtle, supple, almost transparent. One of Da Vinci's many passions was making observations of birds, recorded in his c. 1505 *Codex on the Flight of Birds*, and sketching concepts for various flying machines including his famous "helicopter" and hand glider. One thing is clear: several of his designs prove he realized the way for humans to fly was similar to that of birds, but not exactly birdlike. It turns out that at least one of these designs, his hand glider, actually worked. In October 2005, the U.S. Public Broadcasting

Service (PBS) aired a television programme called Leonardo's Dream Machines, about the building and successful flight of a glider based on Leonardo's design. How did Leonardo conceive and design a glider in the 1500's which could be successfully built and flown 500 years later? By a process we can call Actionable Intelligence Discourse.

Simply put, actionable intelligence means having the information you need to know at the moment you need to know it in order to take action. There are countless examples of actionable intelligence (or A.I., not to be confused here with artificial intelligence). The best and most ubiquitous example is traffic signs and signals. If you are speeding along a freeway at 100 km/h, it is very handy to know when your desired exit is coming up: 2 km...1 km...500 m...etc. Could you imagine the anxiety and potential chaos of freeway driving were that information not made available to you? Now consider how that A.I. is relayed. No matter where you drive in the world, chances are the traffic signs and symbols are kept simple and to the point. Need-to-know information is the order of the day the world over when it comes to driving from point A to point B. What if, instead of this:

you were met with something like this instead:

By virtue of the authority vested in the municipality holding jurisdiction over this motorway, you are hereby ordered to reduce speed in a safe and responsible manner—avoiding if at all possible the shrieking of tires in violation of the municipality's excessive noise laws— and come to a complete stop at the upcoming intersection, proceeding through said intersection only when you have given right of way to other vehicles and it is safe to proceed.
- Motor Vehicle Motorway Act Chapter 115 Article 83. 24-A (ii)
w/Addendum: Municipal By-Law 34.5-12 RE: Excessive Noise

Clearly, our roadways would be an incomprehensible mess were it not for the use of Actionable Intelligence Discourse (AID)—the signs, symbols, and simple labels/phrases that give drivers the information they need when and where they need it.

If you think my stop-sign substitute is an absurdly exaggerated hypothetical example, take this test: go into your files (or online) and review any legal contract you find (such as a credit card agreement or software licensing agreement). Now try to isolate and identify the "need-to-know" information in a moment or two. Have you ever actually taken the time to read the licensing agreement when installing a piece of software? In the world of instant gratification that is the internet (click it, get it), there seems to be an obvious disconnect between the high-speed language of the digital age and the anything-but-high-speed language of law. A legal expert will tell you that everything in a contract is need-to-know information; after all, you need to know exactly what it is to which you are agreeing. But is there no place for a more efficient, effective, yet no less meaningful discourse available by which to do so?

We've all used one kind of hazardous household product or another, and are all familiar with the various warning labels on such products. For example, do we really need to know the exact nature of the consequences of exposing our skin to a corrosive product, such as its molecular composition and the process by which it damages skin cells? The symbol below is all we really need to see to know not to expose our skin to the product—perhaps along with the words "Corrosive! Avoid contact with skin." Any additional elaboration usually focuses on simple instructions for what to do in case of accidental exposure ("flush exposed skin with water, seek medical attention immediately," etc.)

Human beings do have a practical side when it comes to the cause-and-effect nature of our experience. In simplest terms, we evaluate aspects of our life before, during, and after decisions are made, actions are taken, and events unfold. The decision-making process is intended to assess the possible (and probable, if not certain) outcomes of actions and events. Think pros and cons: on balance do the positive outcomes outweigh the negative? The greater certainty in the value of a particular course of action, the more confidence we have in our decision to proceed with it or not. In economic terms, certainty about the future of the economy begets confidence in the markets, which is reflected in higher share values as confident investors put their money where they feel it is certain to grow and/or pay them dividends. Certainty requires intelligence: a reasonable knowledge of causes, effects, and affects.

Knowledge about the outcome of a particular action or event—be it the destination of a freeway exit, the relative safety of a cleaning product, or the potential legal consequences of a contract—is a function of information and time. In any decision-making process certainty requires information, but if that information cannot be made useable within a certain period of time—or is irrelevant given the context of the decision at hand—it may prove to be a hindrance rather than a help. Have you ever heard the terms book smart and street smart? The first refers to a kind of intelligence which involves a lot of information: knowledge well suited to academics and lengthy, complex decision-making processes that, generally speaking, take more time. To be street smart, on the other hand, suggests an intelligence that is based more on knowing through experience and awareness (not to mention intuition or instinct) and is better suited to the hundreds of decisions we make every day of our fast-paced real-world lives. Clearly, an academic approach to gathering, assessing, and applying information is not appropriate in the moment you are trying to avoid a car accident. No one in their right mind begins plugging velocity, trajectory, and other figures into a complex physics formula when the circumstances call for a split-second decision. You simply take action, right? Well, yes and no. Despite the apparent difference between the two kinds of knowing—also commonly known as intellect versus common sense—the reality is that thought does precede almost all action (reflexes aside). Since we have both conscious and unconscious thought, we may not be aware of the thought processes behind all our actions, and this explains how we can feel confident about a certain decision with an intuitive knowing, without actually being able to break down and analyze exactly why we feel so certain about it. Even split-second decisions (like accident avoidance) are made by processing a combination of our conscious awareness of the danger at hand and our unconscious judgment of suitable responses—based on learning, maybe physical training, and, of course, experience.

Are there occasions that warrant a long, systematic process by which knowledge has sufficient time to become ingrained in the minds of the individuals who will be acting on it? For instance, in the case of intensive training programs, what starts out as conscious learning leads to focused practice (including deliberate repetition) and eventually an unconscious knowing—perhaps even mastery—when the activity becomes second nature to individuals. From that point forward, they can act almost instinctively thanks to the extent (and depth) of their knowledge achieved over time—surely this gives them an edge up over others in the same field. This phenomenon is explored in some depth by Malcolm Gladwell in his book *Outliers: The Story of Success*, in which he sheds new light on the old cliché practice makes perfect. By analyzing numerous famous success stories crossing all human disciplines, Gladwell highlights the 10,000 hour rule: that is, a minimum of 10,000 hours spent engaged in a particular discipline is key to an individual's success in that discipline.

There's a difference between learning and mastery, just as there is a difference between knowing in theory and in practice. For instance, let us look at education in science, say, as opposed to military training. The former is a lengthy process of absorbing knowledge interlaced with controlled applications of that knowledge (such as lab work). The latter is a compressed, intensive program designed to provide participants with a near-instinctual practical capacity to respond to combat and other high-stress circumstances. A typical university degree involves four years; boot camp lasts as little as six weeks. In either case, the point is to provide individual participants, not simply with knowledge for knowledge's sake, but rather with knowledge that can be applied in the real world, be it in the lab or on the battlefield, at the precise moment necessary.

If execution is what creates real value and time is money, would it not make sense to always try and provide need-to-know information in the most efficient and effective way possible? I have often thought the most challenging of all communication jobs must be advertising. Whether in radio, television, print, online, or in-store, advertisers have limited space and time in which to make a connection with the target audience—be it conscious or unconscious—and invoke whatever feelings they believe will lead people to take the intended action— buying the advertised product or service. Surely advertisers and salespeople alike can recognize the advantage of making a high-speed connection and a near-digital transfer of need-to-know information with prospective customers. At the other end of the spectrum, anyone involved in investor relations knows that investors have more in common with customers than they would like to admit. With personal experience in both fields, I can say with some authority that when it comes to wanting answers immediately and always being right (i.e., "the customer is always right") investors are as vocal and as impatient as any retail customer. Investors want to feel confident about their investments. Confidence comes through peace of mind—an internal knowing that they're making (or have made) the right decision. Yes, time is money and knowledge is power. These clichés are true in every aspect of business—from investors and management to partners, employees, and customers.

SEE, Show, Tell and Sell Efficiently, Effectively, and Exactly

SEE, Show, Tell & Sell Efficiently, Effectively, Exactly

A natural question arises out of this whole discussion around the concept of SEEing and that is: "What do you mean by Strategy, Engagement, and Execution? There will likely be as many different ideas and definitions about what constitutes each of these elements as there are people in business. For instance, do you include partners and sales channels in the execution of your business? What about the idea of engagement? If you strategize collectively with others within (or beyond) your organization, isn't that by definition an act of engagement? In other words, at some level these divisions and definitions might seem arbitrary and even erroneous to some, and in a very real sense no two managers are likely to SEE in quite the same way. So where does that leave VISUAL AID?

This is my favourite part. This is where I get to make a pitch for the most powerful aspect of SEE VISUAL AID. It doesn't matter; those are just the details. Albert Einstein once said, "I want to know how God thinks; the rest is just detail." So, simply put, don't sweat the small stuff. Over the years I have often found myself telling clients, businesspeople, even academics, "The devil's in the details; so don't give the devil his due." This all might sound trite and more than just a little contradictory, given the focus on "exactness" and "digital communication" advocated above, but bear with me for a moment: if you have come this far down the path to SEEing the light, don't turn back now!

Our conscious experience of the world comes down to shapes and patterns. Just think about it for a moment. We interact with the world, observe and understand it by virtue of our mind's ability to strip away the details of a given set of circumstances while focusing in on the defining parameters—the need-to-know information. Consider one of the most prevalent and functionally important forms in human civilization, the circle (wheel).

Admittedly, there is a fair amount of diversity represented in the above images, and yet our mind's eye can clearly see the dominant functional shape associated with each. Without that inherent ability, our brains could not possibly cope with the physical universe: there would simply be too much information for us to process, classify, store, access, and comprehend. Were we not able to classify a generic shape like a circle and then group specific observations and interactions under that broad classification, our minds would be inundated. Admittedly, there is a lot more to shape recognition (including the logical argument that we know a circle by virtue of it not looking like a square, triangle, etc.); but I too am keeping it simple for your brain's benefit.

Our minds take a similar approach to pattern recognition. In a simplistic way we can think of a pattern as a shape or series of shapes (or sounds, movements, etc.) repeated over and over again. In the above illustration, the pattern that develops is clear: that of repeating circles. We often think of patterns in terms of regular repeating sequences like a heartbeat, the seasons, or even cosmological cycles. However, take a moment to consider some other patterns you may take for granted in your life. Understanding language is all about pattern recognition; even if a person speaks in a cartoony voice or with a heavy accent, chances are your brain will be able to recognize the underlying linguistic patterns and still make perfect sense of what is being said. Consider also this pattern: you get up in the morning, get ready, have breakfast, and go to work. You may modify this pattern slightly day in and day out, but for the most part the basic pattern is the same. Now consider: a bomb goes off in a conflict zone somewhere in the world; one side claims responsibility, the other side retaliates with an attack of its own; it also claims responsibility, adding that its attack was justified...and well, we all know how that particular pattern—the cycle of violence—tends to repeat for years. From the rise and fall of empires to the rise and setting of the sun, our lives are filled with a never-ending sequence of overlapping patterns.

Suffice it to say that the universe as we know it appears to consist of a never-ending stream of repeating shapes and patterns. Whether you look up into the heavens with a powerful telescope and see the swirls of a far-off galaxy, or look down into your ceramic mug to watch the swirls of cream in your coffee, you are likely to find familiar shapes and patterns turning up just about everywhere. In fact, it is fair to say that not only is your understanding of the world based on recognizing familiar shapes and patterns, you instinctively approach new circumstances and unknown territory by recognizing familiar shapes and patterns (and/or identifying and classifying entirely new shapes and patterns), and proceeding with your comparative analysis from that anchor point. For example, when a new astronomical body is identified, the first step is to classify it as a star, planet, moon, planetoid, asteroid, etc. Its characteristics (specific shapes and patterns) determine which primary group, and then sub-group, it belongs to and astronomers label it accordingly. In a more commonplace example, when meeting someone new for the first time, what observations do you make? What questions do you ask them? What are the need-to-know aspects of personality, position, profession, and so forth important to you and your assessment of an individual you meet? Whether you are a homemaker planning a family dinner, a scientist in the laboratory observing results, a lawyer in the courtroom quoting precedent, a CEO of a company evaluating performance, or the president of a country planning the future of the nation, you understand and interact with your world by virtue of your mind's ability to take the infinite number and complexity of overlapping shapes and patterns in any given situation and reduce it to a set of key factors relevant to the decisions and actions facing you in the moment.

As already mentioned, to SEE—strategize, engage and execute—in any given moment is often a function of interacting with other people, which can be understood for the most part as show, tell, and sell. The concept of "show and tell" is fairly straightforward, being one of the first forms of public speaking most children experience in their lives. As far as selling is concerned, it is important to expand the definition beyond commerce to include the exchange of ideas (i.e., selling someone on a theory or a plan of action). To SEE efficiently, effectively, and exactly, means to show, tell, and sell in a way that minimizes miscommunication, misinterpretation, and misunderstanding. VISUAL AID enables a high level of performance, and, in the words of another cliché, is able to put everyone literally "on the same page."

SEE All on One Page

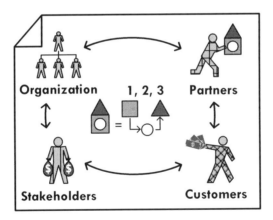

Yet, to put everyone on the same page is no longer a cliché. When you SEE VISUAL AID, you actively participate in the process of overcoming intellectual, psychological, and cultural obstacles that might otherwise prevent you from successfully sharing a vision with others. Rather than having to think about this in abstract terms, it is simpler to think about the process of constructing a building.

Architects make the initial design based on the needs identified by the developers of the project. Based on this understanding of materials, construction, etc. they make certain aesthetic and functional design decisions. Using various visual tools, including design studies (sketches), illustrations, even virtual reality walkthroughs and scale models, the architect shows, tells, and "sells" the vision to the developers. If successful, the next step is to engage the know-how of a structural engineer in the planning and drafting phase. The blueprint will eventually become the "page" that guides everyone on the construction project as they interact with one another and their teams in the execution of the building plan. The blueprint can show everything from structural elements to electrical, ventilation, and plumbing. Without such a visual road map to follow, would it even be possible for us to build the complex structures, machines, electronic gadgets, or software programs that the modern world relies on?

And yet, to the untrained eye, blueprints are not exact. Anyone who has ever looked at blueprints (or schematic diagrams, workflow diagrams, etc.) knows that they are hardly an exact representation of the final product. Even the architect's illustrations appear to capture what the building will ultimately look like better than the simple line drawings of his blueprints, right? But this is the case only from a certain point of view. From another point of view, a photograph or an illustration of the final product is just as inexact. In truth, it is not so much that either is inexact; it's that they are both incomplete. In a 3D universe it is an absolute impossibility to observe the totality of anything at one time. We can see up to three sides of a cube at a time, and only the surface at that. Changing our perspective on anything does appear to alter it from our point of view (i.e., small things that are closer can appear bigger than large things that are far away). But remarkably none of this—neither the inexactness nor the incompleteness of perception—actually fazes us.

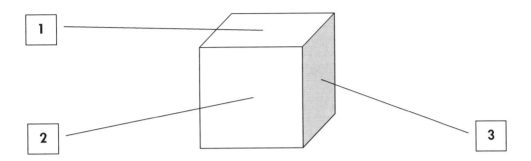

You might think that if no visual perspective can ever completely or exactly convey the totality of the object being observed, our brains might be at a loss. We get along just fine, however. Again, we come back to the idea of keeping it simple. The brain strips away superfluous information in the process of shape and pattern recognition, and fills in (or ignores) missing information in order to understand and interact with whatever is being observed. Just because we cannot see the other three sides of the cube does not mean we question whether they are there (if it's a cube at all). The information the brain is looking for—by way of observation and assumption—is whatever it needs; again, need-to-know information. The construction foreman, electricians, cement workers, and myriad other people working on a building don't need to know what colour the wallpaper in the offices is going to be, nor do they necessarily need an illustration of the outside elevation of the building. The blueprint, on the other hand, is exactly what they need to construct that very same building.

This is an absolutely essential principle to grasp if you are to understand the power of VISUAL AID: that "exactness" and "completeness" are relative terms defined by the ability of all relevant stakeholders to successfully SEE it (Strategize, Engage, Execute). This is what it means to get everyone on the same page; a state of being that opens the door on maximizing value for all stakeholders.

SEE Maximum Value for All

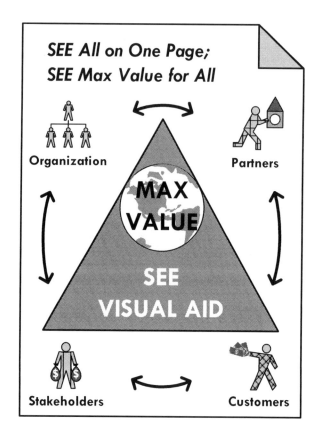

Now that we have walked through how SEE VISUAL AID maximizes value and have seen the process by which VISUAL AID gets everyone literally on the same page, we can add the two together and SEE VISUAL AID's ultimate intention: to facilitate the identification and creation of win-win-win solutions: all on the same page; maximum value for all.

The leap from thinking, showing, and doing more efficiently, effectively, and exactly, to creating win-win-win solutions may not immediately be apparent. This lack is more a function of the general state of mind and real-world practice around these concepts and has little to do with the potential of SEE VISUAL AID. Taken, as one former client of mine put it, as "the most powerful communications philosophy, methodology, and technology [he had] ever seen," the SEE VISUAL AID approach sheds new light on any question, problem, or issue. If we consider it a medium, then we should be able to apply McLuhan's famous axiom, the medium is the message. VISUAL AID uses a spatial and logical understanding inherently universal among human beings. Like traffic signs, blueprints, and many other forms of visual communications, it is designed to transfer knowledge digitally to all who interact with it. Thus, its nature as a medium is one of universal empowerment. What is the definition of a win-win-win? Everyone wins—universal empowerment. If everyone can benefit from the knowledge contained in the medium itself, it follows that the medium is ideally suited to conceive solutions that benefit everyone.

Case Study: A Culture of Collaboration in Healthcare

Common Pulse was established as the online interactive arm of *The Commonwealth Advantage*. According to their website:

> *Recognizing that the Commonwealth's 53 member countries account for 30% of the world's population, 40 percent of WTO (World Trade Organization) membership and about 25% of international trade and investment, the Commonwealth Advantage and CATAAlliance have united to increase Canada's level of economic development, create new trade opportunities and strengthen ties with Commonwealth nations.*

(www.commonpulse.com/about.php)

Common Pulse was to focus on running global webinars (web-based seminars) on various topics and issues relevant to member nations. The inaugural global webinar in 2007 was to "take an inventory of cutting-edge practices in global health care." (www.commonpulse.com/news.php). Since many Commonwealth nations have publicly-funded healthcare systems, this was a particularly relevant topic of discussion, one which would span 24 hours as participants from countries throughout the Commonwealth including Canada, the United Kingdom,

Pakistan, and Australia joined, participated, and left the webinar. Commonwealth Advantage was a client of mine at the time and I was asked to facilitate discussions and record minutes, so that some kind of document could be circulated to all participants after the webinar had ended.

Early into the webinar, it became painfully clear that Commonwealth healthcare directors and administrators were frustrated by the utter lack of collaboration in their field. The nature of public funding means that competition between different levels, jurisdictions, and functional components is fierce, with only one primary source of revenue: the government. The result is that each division or "silo" within the healthcare system goes it alone under a veil of inherent distrust and protectionism, lest their efforts at collaboration and efficiency be rewarded with funding cuts rather than greater mileage from available resources. Regardless, all participants agreed that no model for a *culture of collaboration* in healthcare existed anyway. What could be a better challenge and more valuable take-away lesson than that?

For my own sake, I began by asking the participants just what they meant by a "culture of collaboration" in healthcare. I had already asked the webinar technicians running the event to focus a web cam on the whiteboard in the room where the Canadian contingent had congregated. After some lengthy discussion we arrived at a definition the participants could agree on:

> *A culture of collaboration is defined as a complex, multi-faceted system consisting of semi-independent modules functioning as one by way of a common nucleus containing and communicating a collective vision / goal (life & survival in the environment) derived from a shared blueprint and communicated with a standardized internal / external operating language.*

Now, I began walking the participants in the webinar through what I call *the Attlas Process*, which is basically a way of collective brainstorming and deconstruction. We needed an inventory of the essential elements of the healthcare culture today. "What does the healthcare system look like right now?"

This was a no-brainer, as all the participants were eager to list for me all the components of the healthcare system. Then the follow-up: what the essential elements of a culture of collaboration in healthcare would be. "What would your ideal healthcare system look like?" It was not long before the webinar participants produced a list which included the following elements:

- Canada Health Act (or counterpart)
- One "operable" vision / mission and one common "language" for all members of the healthcare system
- Aggregation of best-practices and progress made to-date in various jurisdictions, silos, etc. made universally available to all parts of the system
- A spirit of partnership, tolerance, trust, adaptability
- National, Provincial, Regional Levels
- Public and Private Sectors
- Public-Private Partnerships
- Vendor Support Infrastructure—collaborative connections between functional elements within the healthcare system and beyond it

Clearly such a list is informative, but it is completely lacking in form. No wonder healthcare administrators had been wrestling with a model of collaboration for decades. Luckily for them, I didn't use valuable whiteboard space to make a list. The participants in the webinar listed the elements of a culture of collaboration in healthcare, while I arranged these elements as shapes and patterns in logical relationship with each other and in no time at all a very familiar and utterly appropriate model began to emerge. The resulting rough VISUAL AID looked something like the reproduction overleaf.

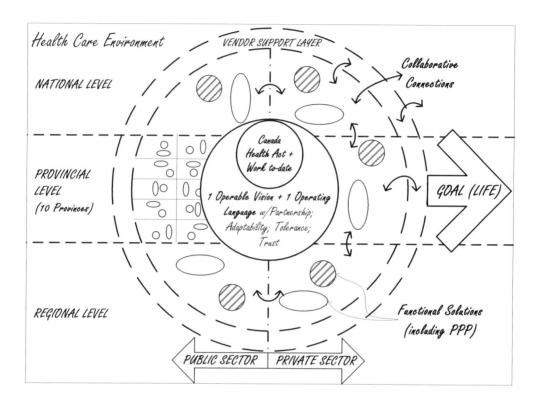

Now, I simply asked "What does that look like?" I added the letters "DNA" and "RNA" to the centre circles (*the nucleus*) and within moments webinar participants in the room and around the world *got it*. Gasps of recognition began to chime in. The diagram on the whiteboard resembled the most fundamental structure of life itself—the living cell. I proceeded to walk through the basic logic of the model. The Canada Health Act is like DNA: the blueprint for all activity in the cell. RNA and protein synthesis transpose information contained in DNA into useable instructions and transports commands to functional solutions throughout the cell (the organelles); a counterpart must be established to do the same for the Canada Health Act. The vendor support layer is like the cell membrane, regulating inputs and outputs between the healthcare system and the environment. The final version of the VISUAL AID that was circulated the next day to all webinar participants can be seen on the next page.

A Proposal for an "Organic Cellular Model" For a *"Culture of Collaboration"* in Health Care

START: Consider the *Nature & Structure of a Living Cell...*

At the risk of oversimplifying, could a living cell be defined as a complex, multi-faceted system consisting of semi-independent modules (organelles) functioning as one by way of a common nucleus containing and communicating a collective vision / goal (life - survival in the environment) derived from a shared blueprint (DNA) and communicated with a standardized internal / external operating language (RNA & protein synthesis)?

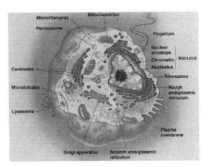

NEXT: Consider the Question of a "Culture of Collaboration" in light of the above definition...

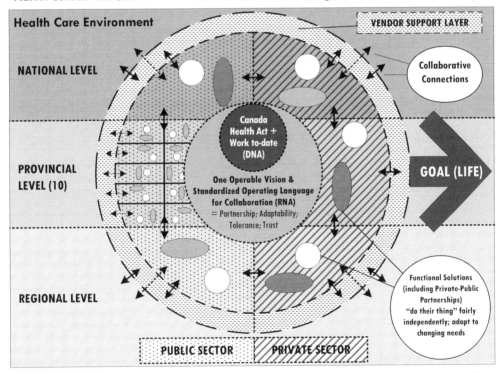

THESIS: *The Medium is the Message;* Health Care need look no further than the building blocks of life to identify a *proven working model* for a living, breathing, "Culture of Collaboration" in Health Care.

The observant will note that I was able to use the webinar's collective definition of a culture of collaboration as a provisional definition of a living cell. This immediately connects the needs of healthcare administrators with the natural world's solution to fulfilling those needs (the model): the structure and nature of a living cell. Now, governments being what they are and given the relative positions of the participants in the Common Pulse webinar (actual frontline healthcare administrators, not legislators), I cannot say for certain that the exercise has produced measurable real-world results as yet. The point of this case study is to illustrate the process by which a SEE VISUAL AID approach can reveal an elegant solution that was staring stakeholders in the face the whole time. One might also see this case study as an exercise in biomimicry—"a new discipline that studies nature's best ideas and then imitates these designs and processes to solve human problems," (www.biomimicry.net). While it did not start out that way, the fact that a basic SEE VISUAL AID approach resulted in a biomimetic model is testimony to the versatility and power of the Attlas Process to create real-world solutions to real-world problems using real-world (including natural world) models.

Again, SEE VISUAL AID benefits all stakeholders, so it is no surprise that the model revealed by the Attlas Process is biomimetic; and if followed, would benefit all stakeholders. After all:

There is no tree whose branches are foolish enough to fight amongst themselves.

- Native American Wisdom

SEE VISUAL AID, the Attlas Process, and the Win-Win-Win

As the healthcare case study illustrates, the Attlas Process, using SEE VISUAL AID, is inherently cooperative, inclusive, comprehensive, and open. It must be if everyone is to benefit from the knowledge contained in the medium, and the medium is to be ideally suited to conceive solutions that benefit everyone. Like so many other examples of visual communications discussed in this chapter, it is designed to transfer knowledge digitally to all relevant stakeholders. The very structure and function of the Attlas Process and SEE VISUAL AID—the medium and its message—is one of universal empowerment—everyone wins.

In my experience, no idea is as powerful and enduring as the win-win-win, be it in nature, society, or the private and public sectors. Human beings gravitate toward openness and honesty—clear signs of integrity—for all human beings seek trust and security, particularly where their purchase decisions are concerned. Just consider the recent consumer backlash against products made in China, thanks to reports of potentially dangerous levels of toxicity, and poor design, quality, etc. Trust is an inherent part of any enduring human relationship and branding is no exception. The strength of well-known and trusted brands—and the good reputations of organizations—can quickly be trumped by negative news reports revealing untrustworthy behaviour, in much the same way that even a rock-solid marriage can collapse like a house of cards when one partner discovers the other has been cheating. A corporation is, more or less, "a person" under the law. In a very real sense, consumers, investors, partners, affiliates, employees, and whole communities have relationships with corporate citizens. The list of corporate "cheaters" hiding unseemly behaviour overseas, off their balance sheet, or underground, is long and distinguished, or rather, undistinguished. If we as human beings recognize that enduring relationships consist of openness, honesty, reciprocity, and balance, why would we expect anything less from our corporations and institutions? Moreover, why would any organization willingly jeopardize its relationship with its stakeholders through dishonest action: a *win-lose* scenario? It's fitting that corporations are seen as persons under the law, for the reasons behind corporate malfeasance are the same reasons why some human beings cheat, lie, advance at others' expense, hurt or kill—greed, ambition, fear, etc. It is fair to say that most of us make a point of avoiding such people.

Not all corporations, and not all people, are interested in advancing at the expense of others, the environment, etc. There is a growing community of social entrepreneurs, activist business leaders, and good corporate citizens intent on building and maintaining strong relationships with the planet based on the idea that the *zero-sum game* is fine for sports, but not for establishing a sustainable global economic paradigm for the 21st century. Bill Gates is very active in this field, calling this new paradigm *Creative Capitalism*. Likewise, there are countless non-profit and non-governmental organizations—and their dedicated members and contributors—whose mandate is to "police" corporations and either report their transgressions or reward them for "good behaviour" with their particular stamp of approval. We will explore this in much more detail in Chapter two: *SEEconomics*.

Notes on SEE VISUAL AID and Volume One of *the Attlas Project*

The SEE VISUAL AID Executive Summary that can be found at the beginning of this chapter is particularly dense and might be more than a little intimidating for the uninitiated. I felt a gradual introduction to the medium, complete with its explanation, would provide an opportunity for you, the reader, to familiarize yourself with SEE VISUAL AID and how it works. You may wish to go back and review it, now that you are well-versed and comfortable with SEE VISUAL AID and the Attlas Process for arriving at win-win-win solutions. I will continue introducing each chapter with its own one-page SEE VISUAL AID executive summary, followed by a more in-depth explanation of the thought processes behind it.

On the question of case studies, I made a conscious decision not to inundate the reader with countless examples of how SEE VISUAL AID worked for clients in the past. The step-by-step walkthrough of the Attlas Process and the healthcare case presented in this chapter was instead intended to lay the groundwork for a forward-looking case study approach: the substance and intention of the Attlas Project itself. If, after completing the book you would like to see more examples of SEE VISUAL AID at work in business, government, and non-profit applications, you can find a portfolio online at www.attlas.ca.

SEE VISUAL AID and the Attlas Process Summary

1. **Strategize (think) with Virtual Interactive Simulation** – Break real-world problems down into their component parts using shapes, patterns, relationships, and logic, measured across space and time, as appropriate. Use visualizations to arrange and re-arrange these component parts, as well as conduct comparative analysis with other entities that appear to share similar shapes, patterns, relationships, etc.

2. **Engage (show) with a Universal Adaptive Language** – Thinking about a problem is all well and good, but ultimately useless if you cannot show your solution and its benefits to others in a way they can quickly relate to. Sometimes you will not have the capacity to strategize without the input of knowledgeable people, and a universal adaptive language (visualization and virtual interactive simulation) is essential for maximizing their collective potential. Literally starting with a blank slate, everyone can participate fully without being hindered by their own language baggage or that of others. Consensus is attainable as participants see an emergent solution materialize before their eyes; they can see their own essential inputs and/or identify with key components of the solution.

3. **Execute (do) with Actionable Intelligence Discourse** – Solving a real-world problem and reaching a consensus on the solution leaves only one thing left to do: make it happen. Using the exact same philosophy, methodology, and technology used in steps 1 and 2 (visualization, interactive participation), simply finalize and polish the record of the process—I prefer one 8 1/2 x 11" sheet of paper—and use it as the basis for building out an action plan (business plan, marketing plan, expansion plan, and so forth). Remember that everyone involved in the execution process must have access to it. They may use more detailed visuals to break out and embellish their specific part of the overall big picture, which need not be circulated, but no one should ever be left out of the big picture.

Social Environmental Economics

START with *Economics as we know it:*

Forces of Social, Environmental & Economic
Progress "Railroaded" by *Business As Usual*

NEXT, *SEE* a New Direction for Business:

1 Vehicle - *SEE Valuation*

2 Platform - *SEE Commerce*

3 Passengers - *SEE Stakeholder Value*

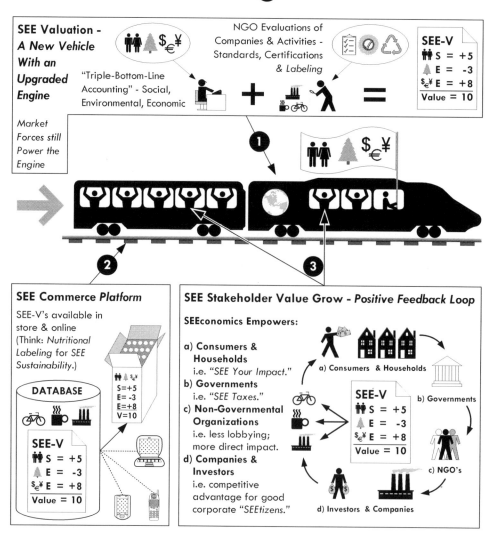

SEE Valuation -
A New Vehicle
With an
Upgraded
Engine

Market
Forces still
Power the
Engine

"Triple-Bottom-Line
Accounting" - Social,
Environmental, Economic

NGO Evaluations of
Companies & Activities -
Standards, Certifications
& Labeling

SEE-V
S = +5
E = -3
$_€¥ E = +8
Value = 10

SEE Commerce *Platform*

SEE-V's available in
store & online
(Think: *Nutritional
Labeling for SEE
Sustainability.*)

DATABASE

SEE-V
S = +5
E = -3
$_€¥ E = +8
Value = 10

S=+5
E=-3
E=+8
V=10

SEE Stakeholder Value Grow - *Positive Feedback Loop*

SEEconomics Empowers:

a) **Consumers &**
Households
i.e. "*SEE Your Impact.*"
b) **Governments**
i.e. "*SEE Taxes.*"
c) **Non-Governmental**
Organizations
i.e. less lobbying;
more direct impact.
d) **Companies &**
Investors
i.e. competitive
advantage for good
corporate "*SEEtizens.*"

a) Consumers & Households

b) Governments

c) NGO's

d) Investors & Companies

SEE-V
S = +5
E = -3
$_€¥ E = +8
Value = 10

CHAPTER TWO
SEECONOMICS

SEE another Definition: Social, Environmental Economics

In the previous chapter, SEE stood for Strategize, Engage, and Execute. In this chapter, SEE will stand for "Social, Environmental, Economic" as in **SEE Valuation** (SEE Value, SEE-V), **SEE Commerce**, and **SEEconomics**.

Accounting for the Tangible and Intangible Costs of Business

One of the interesting concepts in economics is that of *opportunity cost*, the notion that, in free markets, while direct costs of goods and services are contained in the price, one must also consider the benefits of making alternative choices. The inherent scarce nature of resources means that choices are usually based on a prioritized cost-benefit analysis including consideration of opportunity costs.

Consumers, like most entities existing in free markets, have incentives to achieve maximum benefits at minimum costs. While there are exceptions to every rule, on the whole consumers will make purchase decisions based on an evaluation of their choice—the tangible and intangible benefits they will receive versus the tangible costs they will incur, including some opportunity cost factor. Of note here is the consideration of intangible benefits on the part of the consumer. A designer label or prestigious trademark will often fetch a higher price than an identical substitute (minus the mark) despite having the same tangible costs. One might be tempted to argue that supply and demand forces prices higher in this instance, as in others, since designer brands are distributed in limited quantities and the desire to own one of a limited number of units is high. Or a connoisseur might argue that it is precisely the limited availability of premium goods that warrants paying a higher price. In either case, the producers of such goods make up for lower quantities with higher margins. In the case of some producers such as Tommy Hilfiger or the GAP, neither argument applies, since neither of these so-called designer labels are produced in limited quantities. In fact, the intangible benefit of fashion is the very notion of being "fashionable," which by definition stands in opposition to the idea of exclusivity. The paradox of individuality as it is expressed through following the latest fashion trends is a socio-psychological issue beyond the scope of this chapter; nevertheless, the point must be made that markets—especially in the West—have accepted the concept of intangible benefits and use monetary metrics to account for them, despite inherent incompatibilities.

One need only observe the salaries of certain athletes, actors, and CEOs in the West—particularly in the United States—to realize that accounting for intangible benefits with dollars can produce simply outrageous results. Investors and analysts alike have puzzled over exactly how an acquiring firm arrived at the sum paid out in "goodwill." So-called priceless works of art, antiques, and artefacts nonetheless get auctioned off for very real sums of money. The retail price of a designer t-shirt manufactured offshore can sell for double or triple the price of a higher-grade cotton t-shirt "Made in the USA." One cannot deny the inherent incompatibility between intangible value and dollar measurement. Currency is useful for valuating measurable quantities of resources: pounds of salt, bags of grain, kilowatt hours, acres, hours of labour, etc. But how does one quantify the value of the Sistine Chapel or the Great Wall of China? Surely not in terms of square footage! The old cliché "money can't buy happiness" rings true in this regard. Still, markets have deemed it fair and necessary to incorporate intangible value into price.

If there are varying degrees of intangible benefits considered in all economic choices, then it follows that there must also be intangible costs. Like the balance sheet itself, the cost-benefit analysis should balance, and yet it does not. Historically, free markets have over-emphasized the "assets" side and turned a blind eye to the "liabilities." After all, there is no incentive for markets driven by earnings growth and increased profitability to concern themselves with the intangible costs of doing business. The capitalist system, moreover, is ill-equipped to account for intangible costs.

To illustrate, consider a $20 GAP t-shirt. Due to all the advertising and fashion trends depicted in the media, I as a consumer may believe the intangible benefits of wearing a GAP t-shirt (over and above the tangible benefits of any normal $10 t-shirt) are greater than the $10 premium I must pay to wear it. The market has *priced in* the intangible benefits of wearing GAP, and I am willing to pay that price, despite the fact that Costco sells an American-made generic-label t-shirt for $10. The GAP could source t-shirts manufactured under decent conditions, with workers being paid relatively decent wages, and still provide me with a $20 GAP t-shirt at a profit of at least $10. Instead, it sources t-shirts from Southeast Asia manufactured under sub-par conditions, paying sub-standard wages, to provide me with a $20 t-shirt at a profit significantly greater than $10. As a consumer, I have no simple basis on which to make an informed choice in this case, since although the price clearly accounts for the intangible benefits—reinforced through marketing and fashion trends—it fails to account for the intangible costs of GAP's business practices. In short, I cannot readily or easily evaluate all the costs against the benefits.

If I was an investor and not a consumer, I would have an even greater incentive to buy GAP, since its business practices give it a better operating margin, and that translates into higher earnings. Thus, the high social costs of GAP's exploitative business practices abroad and the high environmental costs of its international shipping practices, are reflected in lower economic costs and higher share price for the company and its investors. In other words, the effects of GAP's high intangible costs have been accounted for as tangible benefits—assets, if you will—but the intangible costs themselves have not been accounted for anywhere for what they are—liabilities. Given the natural scarcity of resources and the purported long-term nature of equity investment, such inequitable cost-benefit analysis is unsustainable over time.

Tens of millions of dollars are spent on marketing and advertising the intangible benefits of wearing GAP clothing, but nowhere are the intangible costs mentioned to either the consumer or the shareholder who, by purchasing GAP over another company, are supporting low-paying, high-margin operations in Southeast Asia, increasing contributions to greenhouse gases via shipping, and helping eliminate higher-paying jobs domestically. The ripple effect of their economic choice, compounded with the choice of millions of others following fashion and investment trends, will eventually come back to haunt them, but the effect is so far removed at the time the purchase decision is made it is intangible and unaccounted for—"out of sight; out of mind." Like the billions upon billions in off-balance-sheet debt that caused the collapse of Enron, global markets have set themselves up for a terrible fall. Eventually, all those unaccounted-for intangible costs will catch up to us—this time in the trillions—or if not us, then our children (and/or our children's children).

SEE Crisis in 2008—a Wakeup Call

I believe the current global financial crisis triggered by the sub-prime mortgage debacle in the U.S. and subsequent credit crunch and worldwide recession were foreshadowed by signs which could be seen as far back as a decade ago. What were the cases of Enron, Global Crossing, and WorldCom if not warning signs? These cases of corporate greed, accounting scandals, and outright fraud were the canary in the coal mine that the "prime directive" of Western-style capitalism—growth at any cost—would lead us down a path of even greater financial and market peril. In the ensuing decade, a precipitous rush toward globalization saw the "wild-west" profit culture of the G8 spread like wildfire to the four corners of the world, raising profit growth expectations ever higher. These expectations were piled on top of the towering domestic U.S. economy—the world's largest market and its economic engine—the cornerstone of which was the strength and stamina of the U.S. consumer. For the better part of a decade I watched exuberant business reporters, economists, analysts, politicians, and federal bank chairmen exalt the virtues of the American consumer (that is, the U.S. consumer's seemingly insatiable, unstoppable appetite for spending) and sing the equivalent praises of *hallelujah, our saviour's come!* None of these so-called "experts" showed us the big picture and just how precarious the situation was—and for whom.

A VISUAL AID and walkthrough, *Blueprint for Financial Crisis,* follows below (note: words in **bold-face** correspond with elements in the VISUAL AID.) It may all seem a little overwhelming at first; however, what you can clearly see (indicated by thick, black arrows) are the forces that were at work putting the squeeze on the **U.S. consumer** over the last decade—and over the last few years in particular. International and domestic **profit growth expectations** drove corporate and investment behaviour in the U.S. and abroad, creating market forces **offshore** whose ripple effects hit home for the **U.S. consumer** with a triple-whammy that was utterly unsustainable. I'm no economist; and as complicated as the VISUAL AID may appear, let me make it clear that it's no economic theory, nor does it show all the complex variables contributing to the imminent demise of investment banks in the U.S.—and their subsequent bailout by the government. It is merely a map of the cause-and-effect relationships which contributed to the collapse of the **U.S. consumer** and the credit markets, resulting in the current global financial crisis. That's the irony of it all: the danger was real; if only people were able to *SEE* it.

Blueprint for Financial Crisis

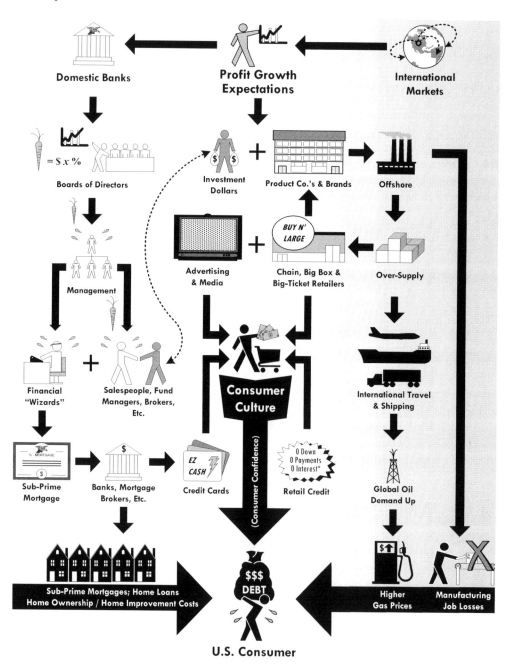

Blueprint for Financial Crisis – *Walkthrough*

International markets were open for business, creating a new "wild west" mentality of financial opportunism (in the "wild east"), which in turn raised **profit growth expectations** among investors everywhere. This led to **investment dollars** and **product companies & brands** making the strategic move **offshore**—where lower costs (due to cheap labour and non-existent social and environmental regulations) meant greater potential return on investment and profit growth. The flood of products hitting North American shores from Southeast Asia exploded, and with this **over-supply** came an explosion of **chain, big box, and big-ticket retailers** together with **advertising and media** relentlessly driving an unprecedented **consumer culture** in order to keep demand up artificially. At the same time, **profit growth expectations** also put pressure on **chain, big box, and big-ticket retailers,** among whom competition became fierce. One in particular, Wal-mart, used its immense buying power to intensify pressure on its suppliers, creating one of the key aspects of what was dubbed "the Wal-mart effect," a feedback loop that leads to even more aggressive **offshore** behaviour by **product companies and brands**. Not only did this unprecedented globalization lead to domestic **manufacturing job losses**—a powerful hit against the **U.S. consumer**—it racked up huge **international travel and shipping** mileage, causing a spike in **global oil demand** and resulting in **higher gas prices** at home—again, hitting the **U.S. consumer** right in the pocketbook. With such "attacks" threatening their way of life (**consumer culture**) one might think that the **U.S. consumer** might have lost **consumer confidence**. **Banks, mortgage brokers, etc.** would come to the rescue, with new and wonderful kinds of **credit cards, retail credit,** and **home loans** to feed the fires of the **consumer culture** and keep **consumer confidence** high by giving the **U.S. consumer** access to unprecedented amounts of **debt**. *Then, unto this camel's back came the straw.*

Back to **profit growth expectations** and the exodus of **investment dollars** to high-return **offshore** opportunities, the **domestic banks** found themselves in a tight squeeze of their own. They had to devise a way by which they could continuously meet or exceed market expectations, both domestically and internationally, and that meant growing their domestic holdings. The **boards of directors** would achieve this with *the carrot and the stick* approach: the "right financial incentives" plus the "right amount of pressure" on **management**. The pressure came down on the **financial wizards** to devise new products to sell to more people, and they came up with the now infamous **sub-prime mortgage**. This gave **banks, mortgage brokers, etc.,** an exciting new product to sell (with commissions—*carrot*) to a whole new kind of **U.S. consumer**, one for whom home ownership was never really in the cards, and who could not afford to own a home (but was convinced by the **consumer culture** and advised by the financial services industry (who are mostly on commission) that it was their "right" and "the smart thing to do"). Once billions in **sub-prime mortgages** were on the books, the **financial wizards** found ways to re-structure and re-package the raw numbers of these high-risk investments into "low-risk" investments (i.e. diversified hedge funds) and highly-marketable, sexy, and pretty much incomprehensible investments (i.e. derivatives) for **salespeople, fund managers, brokers, etc.** to sell (with commissions—a *very big carrot*). This, of course, helped attract **investment dollars** that were bleeding **offshore** back to the good ol' U. S. of A. The plan worked, and many people from senior **management** down the ladder got a lot of carrots as a result.

There was only one little problem: the **U.S. consumer** was already saddled with unprecedented amounts of **debt** and faced ever more **manufacturing job losses, higher gas prices**, and uncertainty. Throwing **sub-prime mortgages** and **home ownership / home improvement costs** into the mix sent the average **U.S. consumer** tumbling. A flurry of defaults and foreclosures snowballed, creating an avalanche of toxic assets on the books of major investment banks in the U.S. and around the world. At the time of writing, the world is still trying to cope with the fallout of the global financial crisis—the worst recession in decades, possibly even since the Great Depression.

SEEing is Believing

To know the risks, you must be aware of them. Herein lies the rub of the whole financial meltdown. Financial and accounting wizards became much more adept at hiding the real risks of the profit-growth culture under layers of clever financial instrumentation—i.e., derivatives and diversified hedge funds—while at the same time finding new and clever ways to sell more and more bank products and services to the American consumer, giving rise to unprecedented levels of consumer debt. A perfect storm of market expectations, business incentives, and consumer culture allowed banks to stretch the limits of traditional lending. No one seemed interested in the big picture; the real risk profile to the U.S. domestic economy: eventual collapse under the weight of all that debt, triggered by job losses and inflation (fuelled by rising energy prices). Markets must be free and transparent—from the board meeting and annual report to the store shelf.

Certainty comes from knowing what to expect: what are *all the benefits* and what are *all the costs* of our choices? Certainty in our knowledge of leaders, governments, corporations, organizations, etc. gives us the capacity to trust their judgment, and the mechanisms they operate on our behalf. Uncertainty usually arises when an outcome is clearly contradictory to that which we expected—an outcome that clearly resulted from factors of which we were not aware (or were not made aware) in the past. As soon as an event like 9/11 shatters the complacency of the population, or a financial crisis like the global credit crunch reveals to the eyes of the public a concealed set of costs that had not been accounted for, uncertainty sets in: trust and confidence erodes; eyes are opened; and minds are awoken.

Honestly, I was not surprised by the events of September 11th: disgusted and saddened, but not really surprised. It was only a matter of time before the intangible costs of U.S. foreign policy came home to roost. In no way do I condone the heinous acts of 9/11 (or any act of hatred or violence), but the United States should not have expected its ongoing policies to pass without some reprisal. Their response—the so-called "war on terror"—is akin to the Roman Empire waging war against Attila the Hun. One cannot win a war against foes that have nothing to lose, especially not when, in their eyes, you have already taken from them all that they could ever hope to want. More recently, Somali pirates have attracted global media attention with violent attacks on cargo ships and bold hostage takings in the Gulf of Aden. Television and YouTube audiences marvel at video-game-like footage of NATO forces running and gunning down pirates at night. This, as the White House ratchets up its rhetoric about getting tough on piracy. A report by the CBC revealed another side of Somali piracy—the fact that most pirates are former fisherman who can no longer make a living due to the illegal overfishing of their country's territorial waters by foreign vessels. While no excuse for violence, acts of desperation are by definition *reactions.*

Anti-globalization protestors at G-8 summits also create great press opportunities—a bunch of left-wing radicals clashing with riot police armed with tear gas makes for good television by any producer's measure. Are these protests really the rants of uneducated hooligans who have nothing better to do with their time than cause international incidents and embarrass host nations and world leaders? Or is it just possible that they voice the plight of a silent majority who cannot speak for themselves—those who pay, each and every day, the intangible costs of "business as usual" by the west?

A Call to Act; an Acceptance of the Difficulties Faced Today

No one can truthfully deny the social, environmental, and economic costs of past and present free-market behaviour; and, to be fair, there are many companies and CEOs with strong ethics and good intentions. There are also numerous products available on the market that represent a better way of conducting business. Whether it be food products sourced with ingredients from non-factory farms, renewable energy systems, or furniture manufactured from tree-farms in South America (not rainforests), consumers have alternatives. But these alternatives are often more expensive and consumers have no simple, easy-to-understand method to account for the intangible costs of their purchases.

Eventually this issue will take care of itself. Economics does, after all, take into account scarcity of resources and supply and demand. The intangible costs of generations of indiscriminate logging, fishing, agri-business, manufacturing, and science and technology will eventually be priced into the handful of fresh vegetables, healthy farm animals, and potable water left on our planet. How ironic if someday mighty CEOs, oil barons, rock stars, and professional athletes must face a future when the wealthiest people on earth are farmers, and a bushel of grain is auctioned off for the price of a Ferrari or a luxury home. Indeed, economics has built in the mechanism—albeit delayed—to price intangible costs into goods, with compound interest to boot.

> *Such an image of the future is "nonsensical," of course. For one thing, the farmers in Canada did not really face the driest summers since the Dirty Thirties these past few years. The "hay trains" departing from Ontario carrying tons of hay to help farmers preserve a handful of animals through the winter must be fabrications—overblown media hype in their never-ending quest for higher ratings via a simple philosophy: "there's no news like bad news." Likewise, the price-gouging of Northern, drought-stricken farmers by their Southern Albertan counterparts (who enjoyed healthy yields of hay that same year) is just an anomaly. True to the economic theory of supply and demand, such a result could never affect foodstuffs. There are no negative effects of global warming; none that can affect us, anyway. The idea that one day green pastures could turn into aerated desert is absurd. After all, ancient lakebeds found in present-day deserts must have dried up so many thousands or millions of years ago that our modern civilization, so varied and complex, is surely immune to such a remote occurrence ever taking place again.*

– The Contrarians and Sceptics

In other words, attempting to account for the intangible costs of business today is an uphill battle. Like the shopaholic armed with a fistful of credit cards (I recall a classic *Flintstones* cartoon, the sound of bugles trumpeting and Wilma and Betty crying out, *"Chaaaaaaaarge-it!"*), it will be very difficult to convince those riding high on runaway free markets of the growing debt (with interest) resulting from their perfectly legal behaviour, to which, they are told, they have "every democratic right." Moreover, since the majority of people lack the capacity to visualize or conceptualize a world so very different than the one they actually live in, talk of change for the sake of survival in the future is either dismissed as science fiction or fear-mongering, and more often than not, is subjected to the death-call of those in power:

> *We are studying the issue, and once those studies have concluded* [years if not decades from now] *we will look carefully at the conclusions and then decide what course of action needs to be taken, but not before then, and not until we know for sure that we have a problem.*

> – The Status Quo "Leadership"

The likelihood of making changes to the free market capitalist system in some fundamental way is very slim indeed. There are simply too many powerful forces that have every incentive *not* to account for the intangible costs of business as usual. There is a loop-hole in the absolute authority of free markets

Forces of Social, Environmental & Economic Progress "Railroaded" by *Business As Usual*

and economic theory, however, a gap through which the silent majority can reach in with a united hand and enact change. This gap is known as social democracy.

The Democratic Mechanisms Available for Change

Many countries worldwide require mandatory nutritional labelling of foods (key health information printed on packaging). Presumably the reason for this is so that consumers can make informed choices about what they feed themselves and their families. There are inherent health risks for those with food allergies or strict diets to consume food "in the dark," as it were. The government recognizes that health risks can directly impact the resource-strapped healthcare system, which in turn, can result in higher taxes. Despite the fact that the franchise-restaurant lobby is a force to be reckoned with in North America and throughout the world, there is a major push on right now in the United States for mandatory labelling and putting health warnings on fast food, as well as taxes not unlike those imposed on the tobacco industry. Eventually, the various social, ethical, and health-care costs of childhood obesity, heart disease, colon cancer, and countless other diet-based health problems must and will be factored into the economic costs of producing, selling, and consuming fast food, just as health costs are factored into the cost of cigarettes. The tobacco lobby was also a powerful one, but not as powerful as the will of a social democracy, which has several vehicles of change at its disposal.

From social activism—boycotting products, protests, civil disobedience—to government intervention—regulations, legislation, taxes—a democracy has within its power the ability to enact change even when faced with the most hardened, entrenched, and powerful of establishments. Mahatma Gandhi demonstrated that millions of unarmed Indian citizens could bring down a regime of well-armed British occupiers using non-violent civil disobedience. On a smaller scale, organized labour unions can effect change in management decisions (although the evolution and present-day status of labour unions is a Pandora's Box beyond the scope of this book). As powerful as the tobacco lobby is, nothing can change the fact that their product poisons people, and therefore the intangible costs of future social and economic stresses on the public must be offset at the time of their purchase and consumption. It may have taken years of feet-dragging by governments and dozens, if not hundreds, of "inconclusive" studies before any concrete action, but the fact remains that even great monoliths of the past can be dragged kicking and screaming down the path of change. Simply put, then, we have real-world examples and models to pursue when it comes to the question of accounting for the intangible costs of business and, indeed, globalization. Nutritional information on food and cigarette taxes are examples of how we, in Canada, recognize an individual's right to know *all the costs* in addition to the benefits of a purchase decision. We believe it is ultimately in the public interest to have intangible costs priced into goods and services, not only as a deterrent and incentive to change behaviour, but as a way to account for accumulating intangible debt that will one day have to be paid back in very tangible ways.

The following section describes, in brief, a potential approach to the issue of determining, communicating, and pricing in intangible costs. They become an integral part of business as usual, thereby making commerce itself a force for social, environmental, and economic certainty, sustainability, and positive change.

SEE A New Direction for Business

If it can be said that the forces of social, environmental, and economic sustainability and positive change have been railroaded by business as usual, then commerce must be brought into alignment with those forces, for the sake of all concerned (for even the most hardened profit-driven individual must concede that a speeding locomotive barrelling down the track at full speed toward *any* obstacle is at risk of being derailed, with disastrous consequences). Sticking to the train analogy, there are three components that must be addressed:

1. **Vehicle** – *SEE Valuation*
2. **Platform** – *SEE Commerce*
3. Passengers – *SEE Stakeholder Value*

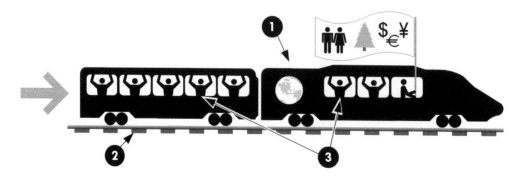

1. SEE Valuation

SEE Valuation is short for Social, Environmental, and Economic Valuation. In principle, the SEE Value (or SEE-V) of a product or service is a compilation of factors related to its sourcing, production, distribution, and parent company. The contemporary models from which the SEE-V was derived include nutritional information labelling of food products, film and television rating systems, selection of companies for so-called "ethical funds," and consumer advocacy groups' product rating programs. The SEE Value is a composite of quantifiable factors as well as qualitative ones. Specific enough that it can be applied to an item as small and simple as a disposable razor, yet versatile enough that it can also be applied to a multinational corporation, SEE-V is not just a clever acronym: it is a practical, useable measure whereby conscientious participants in free markets can SEE the consequences of their economic decisions and make informed choices with much greater certainty.

The logical question that arises from the SEE Valuation proposition is: who does the evaluation? This is in no way a small question. Luckily, we already have models for SEE Valuation, and indeed, organizations and institutions to orchestrate and manage a global SEE Value industry. Government agencies determine the safety, nutritional value, or age appropriateness of products and services. There are also countless not-for-profit organizations and professional associations available to call upon for their expertise and dedication in the matters of health, wellness, safety, security, equality, the environment, etc. Many non-profit and non-governmental organizations already have their own seals of approval. What is needed is not a single operational body to do all SEE Valuation work on its own, but rather an inclusive governing council that can work collaboratively to transmute the *meaning and significance* of existing standards, certifications, and seals of approval into a universal system for SEE Valuation. This body would organize, orchestrate, and manage the contributions of a multitude of contributing organizations in the private and public sector, achieving maximum buy-in and implementation of SEE Valuation.

The beauty of SEE Valuation is that it is completely consistent with the free market ideal of long-term investment. Companies and brands that are in business *for the long haul* have an inherent interest in the long term viability of their business. Such companies tend to have both short term and long term strategies, and in general, they ensure that the latter is not undermined solely for the sake of short term gains: value tends to increase over long periods of time, momentary market fluctuations aside. Companies that take into account the long term implications of their current decisions on the future viability (and value) of their business should—in theory—represent a more attractive investment opportunity for long term investors today. The unprecedented levels of forward-looking knowledge the SEE-V reveals to managers easily translates into an unprecedented level of long-term transparency to shareholders.

This brings us to the second characteristic of SEE Valuation that is completely in line with business as usual. Every publicly traded corporation in North America must submit audited financial statements. Markets rely on the transparency, accuracy, and ethical representation of financial statements to assist in making investment decisions. So important is the auditing process that it is a cost of doing business for public companies. It has created an entire industry (corporate accounting) paid for by the ultimate benefactors—the shareholders. It should come as no surprise that there are already numerous companies participating in *triple-bottom-line accounting,* also known as "People, Planet, Profit" and "Social, Environmental, Economic" (Source: Wikipedia). The triple bottom line (3BL) has its detractors, including Wayne Norman and Chris MacDonald whose 2004 article *Getting to the Bottom of "Triple Bottom Line",* proposes that the 3BL paradigm is a rhetorical device with little substance and may distract managers and investors from more effective approaches to social and environmental reporting and performance. What seems clear is that a key element is missing from 3BL...*SEE Commerce.* Think about it: business only has accounting because there is something to count—money (including assets, liabilities, and shareholder equity)—meaning commerce must come first.

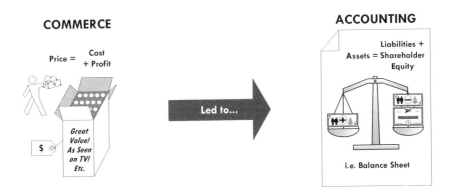

It should come as no surprise that accounting principles like the balance sheet (assets = liabilities + shareholder equity) are more or less derived from fundamental commerce equations (in this case, price = cost + profit). So in order for triple-bottom-line accounting to become a new standard in business, it must have a counterpart at the grassroots commercial level—the foundation of business itself. This is where SEE Valuation comes in. Whereas 3BL accounting (like conventional accounting) is designed to report and communicate the values of a company among management, directors, shareholders, regulators, and prospective investors, SEE Valuation transposes and transmits those values down to the consumer level. Just as traditional accounting is a reflection of the old cost-benefit analysis, triple-bottom-line accounting will reflect the new SEE cost-benefit analysis. Please refer to the VISUAL AID, overleaf.

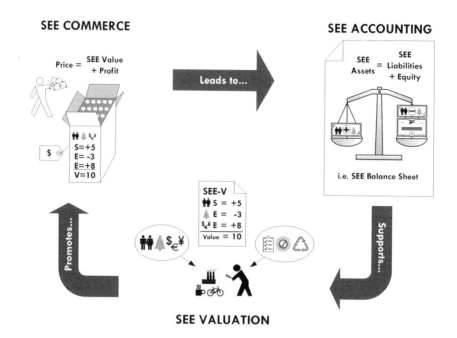

So the vehicle called SEE Valuation needs the platform called SEE Commerce to be truly relevant; luckily, as shown above, the relationship is mutual, symbiotic, and creates a positive feedback loop.

2. Platform: SEE Commerce

SEE Commerce is what happens when consumers have the information they need to make a complete cost-benefit analysis of their purchase decision, at the time of purchase, by virtue of a product's SEE-V. Under SEE Commerce, money is spent based on a value proposition that goes beyond the typical "what's in it for me?" Put another way, the opportunity exists for an expansion of the cost-benefit analysis to include conscious evaluation of

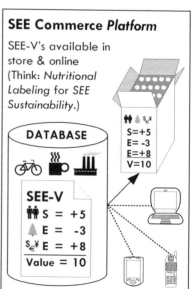

SEE Commerce *Platform*

SEE-V's available in store & online (Think: *Nutritional Labeling* for *SEE Sustainability*.)

tangible and intangible costs and benefits. This is made possible by providing consumers access to information, specifically SEE Valuation information of products, services, and companies. A **database** would house all the relevant product, service, and company information, which could be accessed via the internet through any number of devices. This database would be managed by the SEE Valuation governing council and its member non-profit and non-governmental associations. Companies who participated in the SEE Valuation program would likewise have access to SEE-V information which they would put on packaging and possibly in their advertising as well.

A SEE Value label on a product package or in print advertising might look something like the hypothetical "Widget" example shown here. Now, I can already hear what some critics and naysayers will be thinking, just itching at the chance to tear apart the hypothetical example provided here. The details of the grading system (be it numbers, letters, stars, or something else), how

Widget			XYZ Corp.
SEE Value	👍	👎	**+ / -**
S	10% of profits go to African relief		+ 2
	Pays sub-par wages in Asia		- 4
E	Package made from 100% recycled material		+ 3
	Carbon-neutral operations		+ 6
	Some suppliers operate sub-par standards		- 2
E	Company promotes active shareholder input & involvement		+ 2
	Low reliance on non-renewable energy		+ 6
	Reliance on below-average labour costs unsustainable over time		- 2
	Above average debt		- 1
SEE-V			**+10**

they are calculated, etc. are irrelevant at this point in time. Such details will be worked out via consensus by the NGOs and other organizations that will ultimately participate and oversee the SEE Valuation process. What's important to us in the here and now is to visualize what kind of information a SEE-V label would contain, and make it clear that its intention is to be revealing, but fair.

There will be certain types of products and services whose SEE Value will naturally be below average. Companies providing such products and services must therefore have a means to offset high SEE Costs by making a conscious effort on the plus side of the equation in either the same or another area. In the example shown, the product in question is manufactured under sub-par wage conditions in Asia. This is somewhat offset by the fact that 10% of the proceeds from the sale of the product are donated by the producer to African relief. Ideally, what one might hope for is that "XYZ Corporation" would willingly introduce wage parity. We must accept that certain social, biological, physical, and economic realities will put limits on the ability of companies to reduce or eliminate all SEE Costs. The goal of SEE Commerce is not to eliminate products or product categories (such as snack foods, large vehicles, imported clothing, tropical hardwood furniture, etc.) but to bring the SEE Costs associated with such products and industries to bear on the cost-benefit equation. The positive values represent the company's new "costs of business" that it allocates to offset the sometimes unavoidable negative values. On the flip side, companies that are heavily into philanthropy will be able to provide details about their corporate citizenship to consumers at the time of purchase, and have that giving positively reflected in their SEE Valuation. Consumers might be influenced both by the higher SEE Value and the knowledge of causes they are indirectly supporting by buying from the company. SEE-V labelling would take corporate sponsorship to a whole new level.

From the consumer's perspective, the SEE-V reveals the reality of today and provides a simple and easy way to quickly evaluate and balance the *real* cost-benefit equation of their purchase decision. What's more, the SEE-V gives consumers a substantive new tool in their arsenal of comparison shopping. Since very few purchase decisions take place in a vacuum, the consumer is often faced with making a decision between one or more competitive alternatives. Companies spend billions in marketing, advertising, and sponsorship every year vying for the hearts and minds of consumers. For a good portion of value-conscious people, low price will likely trump most other considerations; however, plenty are far less price sensitive, and a growing number are becoming far more concerned with *values*. The model to consider here is nutritional labelling of food. There are consumers who do pay attention to what they put into their bodies and ones who don't, but giving them the choice by including detailed nutritional labels seems more sensible than not. With the sale of eco-friendly, organic, and fair-trade products on the rise, it's clear that consumers do care, and when given the power to make an informed decision, many choose values over price. It is no surprise, then, that consumers and households constitute the first group of SEE *Stakeholders.*

3. Passengers: SEE Stakeholder Value

If Milton Friedman was right and traditional commerce is all about creating *shareholder value*, then SEE Commerce is all about creating *SEE Stakeholder Value.* Once you embed Social, Environmental, and Economic Values into the bedrock of commerce, market forces simply do the work. Pushed along by the same market forces as before (the intention to create value, competition, growth expectations and so forth), the emergent SEE Commerce activity empowers all those *aboard the train:*

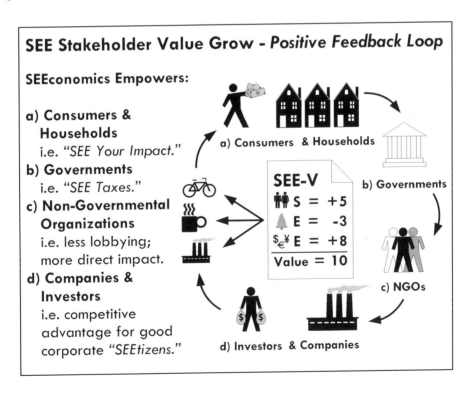

a) **Consumers and Households.** Whether they are choosing light bulbs or selecting an airline, the SEE-V provides purchasers with a quick way to weigh the intangible benefits against the intangible costs—what the SEE Value makes more tangible. Some will point out that consumers already have access to eco-friendly labelling, but a report commissioned by Environment Canada found that only 25 out of 2,000 self-described "green" products in North America were truly eco-friendly. That means 98 percent were "greenwashing"—a term coined by environmentalists to describe misleading environmental claims. Unlike the current crop of disparate eco-labels, a universal SEE-V would be far more comprehensive, less vague, and all but eliminate greenwashing. It should be noted that the acronym "SEE-V" deliberately sounds like "C.V." After all, companies and organizations have used the resume—or curriculum vitae, C.V.—to assess the value(s) of prospective employees for decades. It seems only fitting that people have a similar tool with which to assess the value(s) of companies and their products and services. The difference being, of course, SEE-V's would be standardized and checked for accuracy by third parties. As a result, households could begin keeping a SEE Budget, track the SEE-Vs of the products and services they use, and calculate the impact they are having on the world, beyond a vague notion of "living green" or just adding up their carbon footprint.

b) **Governments.** It's fair to say that tax avoidance is part of the fabric of capitalism, and costs governments (and honest taxpayers) untold billions every year. With SEE Taxation, products, services, and companies would be subjected to a tax rate based on their SEE Value—the higher the SEE Value, the lower the tax. What tax system in history ever rewarded value growth with lower taxes? Investing in SEE Value creation would give companies the double-benefit of increased SEE competitiveness in the marketplace and decreased taxes on earnings. The corporate tax tango currently taking place would take on an entirely different tempo. But domestic issues wouldn't be the only benefit. Products evaluated as having a very low SEE-V (i.e. a high

SEE Cost) could be subject to import tariffs or SEE sales taxes. While behaviour on the part of the purchaser may or may not be influenced by the SEE Value alone, a high SEE Cost priced into the actual dollar price of a good or service will have an effect. This reflection of intangible costs in the actual price of goods and services would not only act as a deterrent to socially detrimental, environmentally irresponsible, and economically unviable corporate behaviour, it would also give governments the ability to collect money from the benefactors of high SEE Costs in compensation for those who ultimately pay the price—people and the planet.

c) **Non-Profit and Non-Governmental Organizations.** These organizations have been, and in effect still are, the caretakers of global capitalism: doing their best with modest means to take care of everything and everyone left behind in the wake of relentless economic growth. SEE Valuation gives organizations active in social and environmental sustainability a means to become embedded in the very fabric of SEE-Commerce itself. Their analysis and information would no longer be thought of (or treated) as a marketing or branding exercise, susceptible to misinterpretation by consumers and greenwashing by unscrupulous companies. Rather, their activities for ensuring complete SEE-transparency for consumers and investors would become no less crucial than accounting and auditing is today, impacting real global SEEconomic change with every purchase decision made.

d) **Investors and Companies**. In no way does SEE Commerce abandon the creation of shareholder value. It simply expands the scale and scope of the very definition of shareholder value. Growing Social, Environmental, and Economic Value is, as we have already seen, completely aligned with traditional views of investment as a long-term proposition. It might encourage some people to know of the existence of so-called ethical funds. These are equity fund portfolios that only include stocks from companies that do triple-bottom-line accounting and cater to the SEE Values of investors. What SEE Valuation and SEE Commerce provide is a vehicle and a platform on which SEE conscious enterprises—and their shareholders—can level the playing field in the marketplace and win some competitive advantage in the near term by changing the nature of the game itself.

Summary

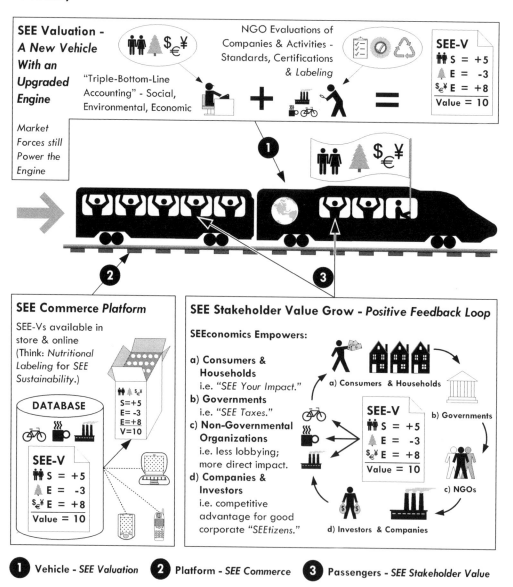

In the long run, everyone wins with SEEconomics. It shifts the economic factoring of intangible costs from the future—when the compounded future value of intangible debts incurred today will cause the collapse of global markets—into the present. Am I suggesting that creation and implementation of SEE Commerce would be an easy endeavour? Not at all; but, at the same time, it is far from impossible.

Call to Action

SEEconomics is not a pipe dream. As I have outlined in this chapter, not only are all the pieces of the puzzle already in place, there is a growing movement around the world calling for change, and a growing number of companies, governments, and NGOs answering that call. If there was ever a time to gather the faithful under one banner and roll out the platform on which to usher in the coming wave of positive change, that time is now. If you are a social entrepreneur, SEE business leader, non-profit or NGO corporate watchdog, philanthropist, social activist, environmentalist, creative capitalist, elected official, government leader, artist, writer, musician, or even just a conscious, concerned citizen and consumer, I encourage you to join the Attlas Project online at **www.attlas.org.** With the active participation of likeminded individuals like you and/or the organizations with which you work, we can hold the first global conference on SEEconomics and take the next step in the Attlas Process— described in Chapter one—for establishing the SEE Commerce Platform and defining the parameters of SEE Valuation. It is a task that may seem daunting, and not for one person or group to undertake, but with SEE VISUAL AID on our side and the right intention in our hearts, we many will indeed act as one, and make SEEconomics a reality.

Society Engaged Electronic Democracy

THE KEY: *WikiPolicy* – REAL Power in REAL-TIME, via Wiki-Technology Similar to *Wikipedia*.

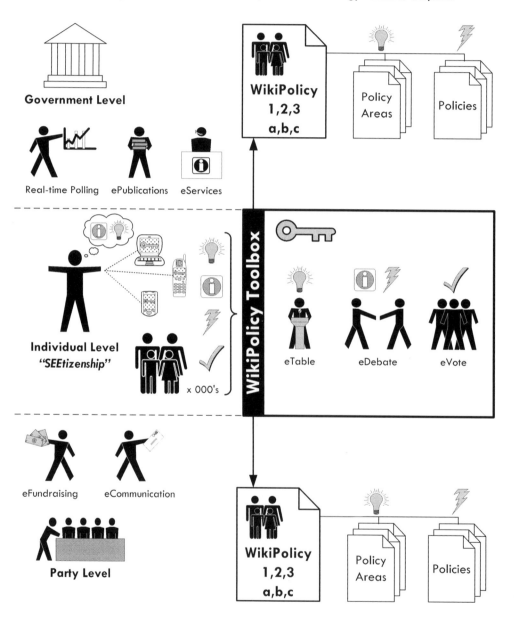

CHAPTER THREE
SEE DEMOCRACY

SEE Another Definition: Society Engaged Electronic Democracy

So far "SEE" has stood for Strategize, Engage, Execute as in SEE VISUAL AID, and Social, Environmental, Economic, as in SEE Commerce and SEE Valuation. In this chapter, SEE takes on yet another definition: **Society Engaged Electronic Democracy** or **SEE Democracy.**

The Time has come for Democracy to Catch Up to the 21st Century

Democracy has taken many forms throughout the years, but it would be overly generous to say that we've come a long way. I personally don't consider the expansion of people's right to vote an upgrade or improvement to democracy, since giving women and people of colour the right to vote was correcting an abhorrent flaw in how the spirit and intention of democracy had been grossly abused by white men in the first place. When I say we haven't come that far democratically, I am referring to the actual intention, structure, and day-to-day functionality of democracy. As an operating system that is supposedly "by the people, for the people," and is intended to support the institution of government, democracy hasn't changed all that much. Once upon a time, the demographics of nations (i.e., literacy and education), coupled with the logistics of mass communication and input into governance decisions, meant having to elect steward(s) of the land every few years and entrusting them with governance of the land and its people; and it made perfect sense. It was a practical, meaningful exercise appropriate to the times. Times, however, have changed; and yet, democracy—in its most basic form—has not.

In this day and age of instantaneous electronic communication and collaboration, does it really make sense for citizens to have their say only once every four years? When the majority of citizens in G8 nations possess a minimum level of literacy and education, with access to media and multimedia information about the issues affecting their lives—globally, domestically, and locally—why should they willingly abdicate their democratic rights to an elected official for a period of four years in between general elections? Once upon a time it may have made perfect sense; nowadays it is a much harder sell. The evidence can be found in the partisan politics being played out within the democratic assemblies of nations worldwide, outside in the streets in front of those assemblies, across the airwaves, over the internet, and so forth. As a voter, you know what I'm talking about: whatever patriotic exuberance you manage to muster during an election campaign—fuelled by the rhetorical promises of the candidates, your own partisan bias, and voting history—often dissolves into helpless apathy months if not years into the term of your elected official(s). Your feelings of helplessness are particularly exacerbated when your elected official(s) vote for purely political reasons—i.e., along "party lines"—for some piece of legislation that has a direct impact on your life, in which you had no say whatsoever. The very fact that you voted for him or her becomes irrelevant, for who could have predicted or known the mind of another human being on some obscure issue that may never even have come up during an election campaign? Sure, you can write to your Member of Parliament, Congress, Senate, etc., but does it really do any good? Why not log onto a website and have direct input into the governance process? Lack of direct, continuous, and meaningful input by the electorate has allowed for abuses of power and full-blown "democratic crises."

Let's look, for instance, at two recent ones taking place on opposite sides of the world.

Democratic Crisis #1: Thailand

At the time of writing, Thailand is undergoing the latest chapter in a saga of dysfunctional democracy. In order to appreciate where Thailand stands today, we need to go back a few years.

February 2001 — Thaksin Shinawatra, a satellite communications mogul, is elected prime minister. He is subsequently charged and acquitted of continuing to manage his family business while in office. Popular with the poor, whom he promises village funds and medical care, he is criticized by the urban middle classes for harassment of the news media and attacks on human rights.

January 2004 — Muslim radicals launch an insurgency in the southern provinces that has so far claimed more than 1,700 lives. Successive moves by Shinawatra fail to quell the rebellion.

February 2005 — Shinawatra is re-elected by a landslide, becoming the first Thai prime minister to serve out a full four-year term. His Thai Rak Thai party becomes the first to win an absolute majority in Parliament. Critics accuse him of using his majority to crush democratic checks and balances.

September 2005 — State-run television cancels a television news program hosted by publisher Sondhi Limthongkul, saying the show that was often critical of Shinawatra was "irresponsible."

November 2005 — Sondhi begins weekly rallies that draw thousands of people and accuses the government of corruption, abuse of power, censorship and mishandling the Muslim insurgency.

January 2006 — Shinawatra's family sells its controlling stake in Shin Corp., the telecom empire he founded, to Singapore's state investment firm, Temasek Holdings, for a tax-free US$1.9 billion. Critics allege the sale involved insider trading and that national assets—including communications satellites—were sold to a foreign government.

February 2006 — Tens of thousands of protesters gather in Bangkok for the first major demonstration demanding Shinawatra's resignation. Shinawatra dissolves Parliament and calls snap elections three years early in an effort to defuse protests and secure his mandate. Thailand's three main opposition parties boycott the vote.

March 2006 — Protesters march on Government House, Shinawatra's office, and vow to stay camped out until he resigns. Other protesters briefly take over Bangkok's main shopping district to send message that Thailand's economy will suffer if Shinawatra stays in power.

April 2006 — Voters go to polls, casting strong protest vote against Shinawatra in election boycotted by the opposition. But Shinawatra claims victory, saying his Thai Rak Thai party won 57 percent of votes. Under increasing pressure, Shinawatra announces after meeting with revered King Bhumibol Adulyadej that he will step down to end the growing protest movement.

April-May 2006 — Shinawatra takes a seven-week break from politics, but returns as caretaker prime minister and struggles to schedule a new election over increasing legal challenges. Relations with senior officials close to king fray.

August 2006 — Shinawatra accuses several army officers of plotting to kill him after police find a car containing bomb-making materials near his house.

Sept. 16, 2006 — Six simultaneous motorcycle bombs kill three people and wound more than 60 on a busy street in the southern town of Hat Yai, an escalation of violence that worsens Shinawatra's deteriorating relations with the military over handling the insurgency.

Sept. 19, 2006 — Military launches a coup while Shinawatra is in New York at the U.N. General Assembly and declares martial law.

Source: The Associated Press
http://www.iht.com/articles/ap/2006/09/19/asia/AS_POL_Thailand _Coup_Timeline.php

2008

29 January — Samak Sundaravej forms a coalition government and becomes prime minister, after winning the majority of seats in the 2007 general elections.

28 February — Former prime minister Thaksin Shinawatra returns to Thailand. He and his wife face charges of corruption.

28 March — The PAD [People's Alliance for Democracy] regroups, threatening to resume protests against Thaksin.

25 May — The PAD begins demonstrations at Democracy Monument, demanding Samak's resignation, and later settles at Makkhawan Rangsan Bridge.

27 June — Samak's government survives no-confidence motion in parliament.

11 August — Thaksin and his wife travel to the United Kingdom, violating bail.

26 August — PAD protesters invade Government House, three ministries and headquarters of the NBT [National Broadcasting Services of Thailand]. Little effort is made to remove the protesters from Government House, although minor clashes between police and protesters are seen.

29 August — Train and air transport are disrupted by PAD supporters, although services would resume a few days later and state enterprise unions would not follow up on their threat to disrupt services.

2 September — Anti-PAD protesters clash with the PAD, leaving 1 dead and 43 injured. A state of emergency is declared in Bangkok, which would last until 14 September.

9 September — The Constitutional Court finds Samak guilty of conflict of interest, terminating his premiership.

17 September — Somchai Wongsawat is ratified by the National Assembly and becomes prime minister. He is rejected by the PAD for being Thaksin's brother-in-law.

29 September — Deputy Prime Minster Chavalit Yongchaiyudh begins negotiations with PAD leaders.

4-5 October — PAD leaders Chaiwat Sinsuwongse and Chamlong Srimuang are arrested by police on insurrection charges filed since shortly after invasion of Government House in August.

6 October — PAD protesters rally at parliament, attempting to block a parliament session in which Prime Minster Somchai is to seek approval of policies. Police attempt to disperse protesters using tear gas. Somchai is forced to cross a fence to exit, while members of parliament are stranded in the building for many hours. Intermittent clashes day-long leave 2 dead and over 300 injured, including 20 policemen. Military troops are deployed to help control the situation.

9 October — An appeals court withdraws insurrection charges against PAD leaders and releases Chamlong and Chaiwat on bail. The following day, The remaining PAD leaders turn themselves in to police and are released on bail.

21 October — The supreme court finds Thaksin guilty in a land purchase conflict of interest case, and sentences him to two years in prison.

8 November — The Government of the UK, where Thaksin had been primarily residing, revokes the visas of Thaksin and his wife Pojaman.

25 November — The PAD blockades Don Mueang, where the government held its temporary offices, and Suvarnabhumi International Airports, leaving thousands of tourists stranded and cutting off most of Thailand's international air connections. Several explosions and clashes occur in the following days.

2 December — After weeks of opposition-led protests, the Constitutional Court of Thailand dissolved the governing People's Power Party and two coalition member parties and banned leaders of the parties, including Prime Minister Somchai Wongsawat, from politics for five years. Wongsawat promptly resigned.

2009

11-12 April — The UDD [National United Front of Democracy Against Dictatorship] protest group stormed the Fourth East Asia Summit in Pattaya, forcing its cancellation. Prime Minister Abhisit Vejjajiva declares a state of emergency in Bangkok and five neighbouring provinces.

Source: Wikipedia
http://en.wikipedia.org/wiki/2008%E2%80%932009_Thai_political
_crisis

April 20, 2009 — Bangkok was under a state of emergency for a ninth day on Monday to contain political violence that has seen troops clash with protesters, and an assassination attempt on the leader of the royalist pro-government movement. Prime Minister Abhisit Vejjajiva has said it will stay until he is sure red-shirted supporters of former premier Thaksin Shinawatra have abandoned their anti-government protests.

Source: Reuters
http://www.reuters.com/article/latestCrisis/idUSSP434712

What one constant runs through Thailand's turbulent, "revolving door" democracy? The same thing that hinders government here in the West: the struggle for power.

Democratic Crisis #2: Canada

Like Thailand—and many other countries around the world that were once British colonies and are now members of the Commonwealth—Canada is a parliamentary democracy. This essentially means that Canadians do not elect a prime minister so much as they elect a political party to occupy the majority or minority of seats in the House of Commons. Citizens in each riding elect a member of parliament for that riding. When the votes are tallied, whichever party has won the most seats—that is, the most members of parliament elected in their ridings—is said to have the mandate of the people and forms the government. The leader of that party—as selected by its delegates prior to an election—is then formally installed as Prime Minister by the Governor General, who is not only the Queen's official representative in Canada's constitutional monarchy (harkening back to Canada's days as a colony within the British Empire), but is titular head of state under the constitution. Her powers are prerogative, however, meaning she is there not to govern the nation—that is the role of parliament—but to govern parliament itself, though only during times of constitutional and political impasse. For example, the Governor General can dissolve a dysfunctional parliament, call a general election, and even oversee the transfer of power between sitting blocks of members of the House of Commons. Such cases are rare and to date no Governor General has ever had to oust a sitting Prime Minister (although the latter have resigned due to impasse with the Governor General). But Canada's current Governor General, Michaëlle Jean, and Prime Minister Stephen Harper did recently set a new historic precedent.

Prime Minister Stephen Harper's minority Conservative government faced imminent defeat in the House of Commons on a confidence motion they presented for the first time on November 25, 2008, in which they failed to provide any details on an economic stimulus package to address the effects of the global financial crisis (discussed in Chapter two). They did, however, announce a plan to cut public funding to political parties—a move innocuous to the Tories, flush with cash, but disastrous for the other political parties, all struggling with their finances. Well, it didn't take a rocket scientist to figure out that the opposition were not going to support such a motion by the government and that they would pursue a non-confidence motion to topple the Conservatives, despite the fact that Canada had just finished going to the polls a month or so earlier. Perhaps Harper thought the threat of plunging the country into another unwanted election would be enough to keep the opposition in line—particularly the Liberals, whose then lame-duck leader, Stéphane Dion, wasn't to be officially replaced until a convention in May 2009. Or perhaps Harper, unsatisfied with a second minority government in as many elections, wanted to force an election in an effort to win more seats. One thing is certain: the move was brazen and provocative, and the counter-move by the opposition was no less so.

SEE DEMOCRACY

Approximately 65% of Canadian voters hadn't voted for a Conservative Member of Parliament. The makeup of the House of Commons saw the majority of seats going to the Liberals, the New Democrats (NDP), and the Bloc Quebecois (Bloc), a regional party representing the interests of the province of Quebec (including, they claim, Quebec's desire for sovereignty). The reaction of these parties to the Conservatives' provocative move was to sign a coalition agreement. Under the terms of the agreement, the Liberals and New Democrats would form a coalition government, with cabinet positions held by both party members—and Dion would be Prime Minister until May 2009. The Bloc would not officially be members of the coalition government, but would agree to support the coalition on confidence motions in the House for a period of 18 months. Reaction to the coalition agreement was swift and fierce, with Harper claiming (incorrectly) that the coalition did not have constitutional authority or a mandate from the people, and that Dion could not become Prime Minister without first being chosen by the people of the country. Constitutional technicalities aside, the reaction of Canadians was also swift. Within hours of the announcement there were at least three Facebook groups, one with nearly 5,000 members by the end of the week, all declaring "No Coalition Government." Opinions on the street seemed mixed, however, with some people saying that perhaps a coalition government might do better than another term of Conservative minority rule. One thing is clear: no issue or political situation seemed to electrify the Canadian public as much in recent history, not least because, with the ball back in the Harper's court, he turned to the Governor General to make his next play—a power play at that.

On the morning of December 4, 2008, the Prime Minister's motorcade pulled up in front of Rideau Hall in Ottawa, the residence of Her Excellency Michaëlle Jean, Governor General of Canada. In a meeting that was supposed to last only a few minutes, but stretched to over two hours, the Prime Minister advised the Governor General to *prorogue* Parliament—a fancy term for putting the session on hold—until January 27, 2009. Never before in the history of Canada had a sitting Prime Minister, faced with imminent defeat in the House of

Commons, asked the Governor General to suspend Parliament. It is clear that granting such a request could set a dangerous precedent, and yet, that is exactly what Ms. Jean did. Parliament was put on hold, Stephen Harper effectively cashed in a "Get out of Jail Free" card courtesy of the Governor General, and now the real circus act of Western partisan politics was under way, just in time for the holiday season.

The Conservatives had already begun running election-style television attack ads in the week of the coalition announcement. After Parliament was put on ice, Dion stepped aside as leader, making way for Michael Ignatieff to take on the position. In a television interview which aired December 10, 2008 on the Canadian Broadcasting Corporation's National newscast, Harper expressed his intention to work cooperatively with the new interim Liberal leader and the other leaders of the opposition. As it turns out, the coalition agreement between opposition parties didn't last the prorogation period. Of course, neither did Harper's contentious clause that would have yanked political party funding. It appears that Harper's unprecedented move paid off. Not only did his government live to see another day, he gained time to repackage his economic stimulus plan into the annual Federal Budget. The political wrangling didn't go away, however, and in a speech made March 10, 2009, Prime Minister Harper said he was "very frustrated with the opposition parties" who are using "political red tape" to stall rapid adoption of a crucial budget (economic stimulus included).

It remains to be seen if talk of a coalition will re-surface. One thing is certain: flush with cash, the Conservatives are in a good position to launch a propaganda campaign unlike any we've seen against any coalition attempt to seize power, be it over the budget or some other issue. The beleaguered Liberals—new leader notwithstanding—and their would-be coalition partners the New Democrats will strike back as best they can with the Bloc, who—as a separatist party from Quebec—can only add fuel to the volatile fires of division. After all, the majority of the Conservatives' seats are in Western Canada, and there is no love lost between Alberta and Quebec, especially since the highly divisive National Energy program was brought in by the Liberals years ago. With a majority government made possible by holding many seats in Quebec, the Liberals brought in a program that requires Alberta to share valuable oil revenues with the rest of the country. In a coalition scenario, with a separatist party from Quebec holding the balance of power on key issues, Westerners might again feel their democratic rights being sidelined by Central and Eastern Canada. No doubt the Conservatives will play up these divisions (and fears) to their advantage. In numerous televised speeches, Stephen Harper made an appeal for opposition parties to work together with him and not toward the blind pursuit of power. How ironic, when it is precisely the preservation of power that is foremost on Mr. Harper's agenda.

The Problem with the Pursuit (and/or Preservation) of Power

In late December of 2008, Greece had seen weeks of rioting by so-called anarchists, youth, and university students sparked by the shooting of a teenage boy by Greek police. It was a shame to see the land that gave birth to modern Western democracy burning in the flames of anger and resentment by a mass of people accusing the government of being run by the elite, for the elite.

I wonder what it is about the concept *by the people, for the people* that many contemporary political parties do not seem to be able to grasp. I don't know by what logic or rules of grammar that politicians can take such an eloquent statement and interpret it as *by the people, for us*—"us" being whichever elite group's interests they represent (if not entirely their own self-interest). I think you'd be hard pressed to make a reasonable objective argument that the vehement partisan power struggles that take place the world over—including the examples outlined in this chapter—are in the interests of the people. Don't get me wrong: they take place in the name of the people; and, with hundreds of years of practice and tradition, even garner the passionate support of a good number of the people. In the context of the 21st century, however, partisan politics and the majority of so-called democratic power struggles cannot make the claim that they are by the people, for the people. They are, instead, the side-effects of a hybrid governance scheme from another era, one that fused (and confused) true democracy with elitist notions and imperial traditions about who should be allowed to govern and how often they need to turn to the people to renew their mandate. I admit this is a harsh accusation, but let's take a closer look at what we know as democracy.

Every few years, those of voting age among the populace are permitted to put an "X" in a box, indicating their preferred choice for governor—I will use the term "governor" here as a generic term to refer to every type of elected official, from mayor to member of parliament to president. This occasional call for direct input from the populace enables (and encourages) the formation of competing factions (usually nationally) who jockey for power. During an election campaign, they can effectively say or do whatever is necessary to woo voters; once elected—and given a strong enough mandate—they more or less have free reign to do as they please. The result is an endless list of unsubstantiated claims and broken promises by successive administrations, some of whom inevitably face the anger of a population that feels betrayed. In the West we may think our democracies are more stable, with more checks and balances to prevent abuse of power. But make no mistake: just as in Thailand, Greece, and elsewhere around the world, there is precious little standing in the way of a Western government to act as it chooses except for public protests, civil disobedience, and/or direct violent intervention/insurrection—which we often see taking place in other democracies around the world. It should be noted that in the United States, one of the world's best-known, most stable, and most powerful democracies, "anti-terror" laws have been passed since 9/11 that effectively give the government legal authority to take measures against any such popular uprising. In Canada, the government has the power to invoke the War Measures Act, as it did during the FLQ crisis in 1970. It is not my intention to list similar provisions on the law books of democratic nations around the world before and since 9/11. Suffice it to say that governments are periodically elected by the people under some pretence, then rule more or less unchecked, with powerful tools at their disposal to defend their position should a popular uprising ever threaten their power and authority.

Dr. Wayne Dyer, American psychologist, author, and self-help guru, had an interesting take on the idea of elected leaders. Imagine hiring some people to come into your home to take care of the house and manage your affairs for you. You interview a few candidates and pick the best ones based on their experience, abilities, etc. Then, shortly after hiring them, they turn around and begin changing the house rules and making major life decisions on your behalf. When you question their choices and decisions, they assert their authority over you, your family, and your home proclaiming it was you who chose them to "lead" you; and, that you will have to wait four years before you can fire them. Oh, and by the way, the house rules, regulations, and programs they bring into effect may or may not be their own (they may even go against their own consciences) but are based on the tenets and philosophies of the "parent company" (political party) of which they are members. Now, anyone can see the absurdity of this kind of arrangement, yet on a national level we call it democracy. On a philosophical level we herald it as the best form of governance available to us.

What else happens during the four years between scheduled elections? Bickering, arguing, and petty squabbling; endless debate in assemblies, on airwaves, and on the internet; and lots of talk about what should and shouldn't be done, with relatively little action. Coming back to the household analogy, you hire people to manage your affairs and look after your home, not sit around in the dining room debating with one another about what needs to be done. You are said to have "freedom of speech" and can write your member of Parliament/Congress to complain, but in fact the only public input that ever makes it into the official debate between political parties are those well-worded arguments that happen to support a particular agenda. In an election campaign, politicians on opposite sides of the so-called political spectrum are in a contest to win power. Between campaigns, they are in a contest to undermine each other in a bid to position themselves at an advantage in time for the next election (and make their elitist supporters and lobby groups happy by quietly passing laws in their favour). If this sounds far too cynical, watch the political news in your country for one week.

It is not my intention to criticize or judge the people who believe in the institution of democracy or those who sign on to be members of Parliament, Congress, Senate, etc. There are certainly some noble, kind-hearted, right-minded individuals who enter politics with the intention of making a difference or making their country (and their world) a better place. The problem is not that the majority of people in government are corrupt. The problem is that they are locked within a power contest whereby in order to make a difference they must win and preserve power. Like some modern-day version of a Roman gladiator, today's politicians can win their freedom (and then be able to make a difference), but, as in the Coliseum, at what cost of human life and limb?

In Chapter two we looked at economics not as being "wrong" in so much as being "incomplete." Focused on profit growth, ignorant of intangible costs, the nature of the system itself is corrupt and corrupting. Participants are implicated in the wholesale destruction of social and environmental values, not because they are corrupt people, but because the system itself gives them few means by which to act in a balanced and conscientious way. The consequences of their economic decisions are kept out of sight, out of mind—they act in the dark. SEEconomics changes that. Now consider democracy from this same logical framework.

Democracy is not a bad idea; its current form had its time and place, and was arguably superior to alternative forms of governance. In its contemporary form, however, democracy's focus is on the pursuit and preservation of power, and this fact forces politicians—who are not inherently corrupt, competitive, or divisive—to participate in a contrived game of competing ideologies focused on jockeying for control rather than fulfilling their fundamental mandate as stewards chosen by the people to serve the people. Democracy, like economics, is not wrong, it's just incomplete. Let's *SEE* if together we can complete the picture and make it all that it was intended to be.

SEE Community – Society Engaged Electronic Community

The internet has changed many aspects of our lives. Technology has opened the door to interactivity and collaboration in areas that were considered the domain of the elite for centuries. YouTube effectively allows anyone with a computer and a webcam (or perhaps a smart phone) to broadcast to the world. A generation ago, buying and selling stocks was not a mainstream activity, and so-called day-traders were a rare breed. Today, vast numbers of people buy and trade stocks, commodities, and currencies online without ever speaking with a broker. At last count, Wikipedia claimed to have over 2,847,000 articles in English, dwarfing the once iconic *Encyclopaedia Britannica*. To those who might argue that knowledge is about quality, not quantity, it should be noted that the user-moderated and edited Wikipedia has produced a relatively accurate and robust knowledge base, considering that contributors receive no financial compensation. This is perhaps one of the most interesting and powerful aspects of online technology and the internet phenomenon—especially wiki technology.

The impetus to contribute one's time, energy, and talents toward the common good is a phenomenon that is ingrained in all of us—it is called community. Organized religions try to take credit for this. Their leaders argue that working toward the betterment of life for "the group" and for individual members within the group can be attributed to religious beliefs, traditions, and value systems. But it is interesting to note that one of our closest genetic cousins in the animal kingdom, chimpanzees, exhibit a similar level of care and compassion toward others they identify as being members of their community. Like human beings, chimpanzees tend to be xenophobic, protectionist, and even hostile toward members of other groups. In theory, if chimpanzees were able to form a large enough group—identifying kinship with any and all other members of their species all over the world—they would no longer hold any hostility toward any other chimps, and revert to their natural caring, compassionate state. I believe this is precisely what has happened with the internet in general and sites like YouTube and Wikipedia specifically. The internet allows for the free flow of information and interactivity—the two essential components of relationship building. As human beings spend more time exchanging information and developing relationships in a domain free of national borders, economic strata, even academic boundaries, they recognize a universal kinship that exists between them. Traditional differentiators (age, sex, race, religion, nationality, etc.) do not disappear, but they seem less relevant in online spaces that are more about sharing ideas and experiences that bring us together versus defining that which keeps us apart. Isn't this what generations of human civilizations have come to know as community building? A collection of people who still have many differences—for no group of human beings are a set of clones—identify themselves as members of a larger whole based on a set of affinities. Individuals then give of themselves for the benefit of the whole group and all its members.

Wiki-Community

Recalling Marshall McLuhan for a moment, the medium really is the message when it comes to the internet, especially as it applies to the wiki, as in Wikipedia. A basic definition states:

> *"A Wiki is a type of website that allows the visitors to add, remove, and sometimes edit the available content. This ease of interaction and operation makes a wiki an effective tool for collaborative authoring."*

Source: http://groups.involving.org/display/STR/Glossary

Based on what we understand as authoring—the writing of a document by one person (or a handful of individuals) for the benefit of many—collaborative authoring means writing a document by many individuals for the benefit of many. The nature of the document itself, however, is relatively unchanged. That is, collaborative authoring doesn't produce a unique version of a document for each contributor (that would defeat the purpose); rather, collaborative authoring produces a single version that represents the collective creativity, imagination, wisdom, intelligence, and talents of its contributors. Not only that, the process of collaborative authoring requires consensus and agreement by default. Critics will argue that this attribute makes for "art by committee" and thus "bad art," but where non-fiction and other documents of practical daily use are concerned— i.e., knowledge bases in business, science, etc.—a wiki approach is ideal. It is no wonder intranets are so common in business and academics. While most of these are closed systems, limiting collaboration to authorized members of a specific organization, they nonetheless operate on the principles of open networking, collaboration, and the spirit of community, i.e., *we're all in this together.*

I am reminded of that famous cry of solidarity and brotherhood from literary tradition: *"One for all, all for one!"* When Alexander Dumas enshrined those words as the battle cry of his iconic three musketeers, I wonder if he could have imagined its relevance in the technological age of the 21st century. For truly we would be hard pressed to find a more aptly fitting expression of the spirit of wiki technology and its applications, including Wikipedia—one repository of knowledge made by all, for each one of us. Just consider this: never before in the history of human civilization have so many human beings been able to participate so directly in the creation of one thing for the benefit of all. Certainly projects like the Great Pyramid and the Great Wall of China may come to mind; some might cite the Second World War or even the Manhattan Project, but let us remember the rather inauspicious circumstances under which these monuments and events of human history came into being. Until the internet came along, there was no truly global project whose intention had nothing to do with "us versus them" or the sum-zero game. Not only does the internet make Wikipedia possible, it proves that consensus and agreement on a global scale is not only feasible, it is a natural evolution that flows from the medium itself and requires no official oversight. Again, that oversight is simply built into the medium. This ensures no one individual (or small group of individuals) is either responsible for, or able to unduly benefit from, the project. Everyone wins. And really, isn't that what the nature and intention of community is supposed to be all about?

Wikipolicy

As already discussed, what we know as democracy first came to dominate the West when access to education and communication technologies meant people had little choice but to elect educated, articulate individuals who would speak for them, argue on their behalf, and install their vote by proxy. After much argument, debate, and official vote, these elected officials would produce some form of proclamation that became the law of the land to which all citizens were henceforth beholden. The opportunity presented by wiki technology is to put an end to this pattern of democratic displacement and power by proxy. With *Wikipolicy,* the people have direct input into the legislative process. Individuals exercise a more active form of *"SEEtizenship"* (Society Engaged Electronic Citizenship) by being hands-on in the decision making process that determines the policies of their nation and its course for the future. The limitations of education and communication that produced the versions of democracy to date are solved by Wikipolicy—the multimedia technology it runs on is inherently interactive, informational, and connected to the internet at large.

Wikipedia has demonstrated the ability of individuals to collaborate at a global level on a resource for use and benefit by all others. But when we talk about a wiki-based resource for governmental direction—Wikipolicy—we don't have to talk on a global scale. In other words, although Wikipolicy could theoretically provide a global platform for governance, more than a few established states will want to preserve their sovereignty and autonomy. This is a reflection of the fact that, despite having national assemblies and federal governments, most nations also have multiple additional governments overseeing regional and local jurisdictions (i.e., state, provincial, and municipal). Given any geographically and culturally diverse society, there is a practical limit to the number and nature of decisions that can be made centrally. That said, just as representative democracy is the preferred model worldwide for governance at every level, so too Wikipolicy can serve as the technology infrastructure that supports governance at all levels. Instead of one massive Wikipolicy for everything, multiple Wikipolicies would oversee specific towns, regions, nations, etc. As an example, even Wikipedia consists of multiple wikis written in different languages, each operating more or less independently of the others (this accounts for the variance in number and type of articles by language). Finally, using Wikipolicy to support existing democratic systems and structures does not preclude applying it to the bigger picture and larger questions of humanity and our planet as a whole. In terms of the United Nations, the Universal Declaration of Human Rights, and other such "humanity-in-totality" applications, Wikipolicy can facilitate empowering human beings to play an active role on the world stage.

Future SEEtizens will not only be extremely comfortable working with the Wikipolicy platform—local, regional, national, and global—*they will demand it.* An entire generation has been raised with a world of information and unprecedented communication technologies available to them at their fingertips, a trend that has quickly spread worldwide. It is this on-demand aspect of technology that is fundamentally empowering and will continue to produce more empowered and conscious individuals who will want to control their own destiny. Like any do-it-yourself oriented person, SEEtizens will reach for the tools and technologies with which they are familiar to get the job done.

Wikipolicy Toolbox

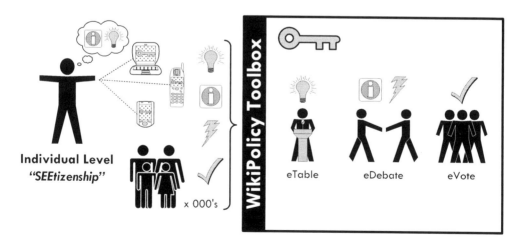

At the **Individual Level**, it's actually as simple as it looks. Wikipolicy is all about empowering citizens to become truly active and connected, creating a whole new kind of *"SEEtizenship"*. The key is the **Wikipolicy Toolbox** that gives hundreds of thousands of individual SEEtizens (and their families) the ability to electronically table, debate, and vote (**eTable, eDebate, eVote**) on specific solutions, issues, laws, etc. As they can do this from anywhere they have internet access (including a growing number of portable devices), they can always feel connected with the decision-making process and more in control of their lives. Like checking their email, they can check on what progress is being made on the issues relevant to them: personal, family, community, country, and the world. Parents and teachers can involve children in the process, who have been held as political prisoners for far too long by governments who have given them no respect and zero input in the policy-making of today while at the same time burdening them—their futures—with the consequences of today's often short-sighted decisions. In its most basic form, Wikipolicy is an enabling technology producing more connected and proactive SEEtizens engaged regularly in the legislative and decision-making processes of governance. Of course, there are a lot of technical and procedural details behind this basic model, and such details are best left to the technical, legal, and constitutional experts within each legislative jurisdiction implementing its own Wikipolicy platform.

So where does that leave political parties and the traditional workings of democratic governments? Should they feel threatened? Are politicians and parties a dying breed in the wake of Wikipolicy technology? Wikipolicy cannot eliminate government and politicians any more than Wikipedia can eliminate academics and professors. The reason I refer to Wikipolicy as a "toolbox" is to emphasize that it is at the service of people: it enhances and empowers society— all of society. Remember, SEE Democracy, like SEEconomics, is derived via the Attlas Process using SEE VISUAL AID, which means that it fundamentally supports everyone: the win-win-win. No one is left out. That includes the lawmakers and leaders of today and tomorrow.

SEE Political Parties

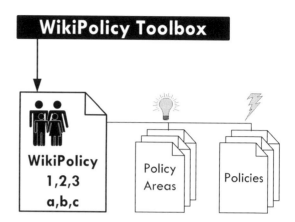

People who share common beliefs and agendas naturally gravitate toward one another to form groups, and the numerous internet social networking sites are testimony to how technology enhances the exchange of ideas among such individuals. So, at the political **Party Level**, Wikipolicy is not a threat but a valuable asset, helping shore up the active participation of existing members, while at the same time attracting new members with an open and inclusive approach. By reducing back-room wheeling and dealing, political parties can hope to renew their status in the minds of cynics, disengaged citizens, and disenfranchised voters who have long since abandoned partisan politics. Wikipolicy allows political parties to provide an online space for concerned citizens to be more proactive and become positive contributors to a movement of like-minded individuals. Not only that, nothing can compare with inclusive interactivity when it comes to educating the public.

> *Tell me and I will forget, show me and I may remember, involve me and I will understand.*
>
> - Chinese Proverb

In recent years, the Internet has emerged as a major tool for political parties in terms of **eCommunication** in general and **eFundraising** in particular. With each passing year, political parties around the world are becoming more and more sophisticated when it comes to using technology to spread their message, attract supporters—campaign contributors and volunteers—and generally organize and run their operations. The cover story on the April, 2009 edition of *Fast Company* magazine featured "The Kid who made Obama President: How Facebook Cofounder Chris Hughes Unleashed Barack's Base—and Changed Politics and Marketing Forever." If recent examples in online politics are any indication, adding another layer of technology to the mix should not be a challenge given the current level of sophistication. Besides, the nature of wiki technology means that once it is up and running, it pretty much runs itself. Now, consider the explosive popularity of interactive online communities, from Facebook to YouTube to Second Life. The political party who gains first-mover advantage on the Wikipolicy front may find itself with an overwhelming value proposition to voters and a competitive advantage to match. In short, political parties stand to benefit immensely from embracing Wikipolicy and transforming themselves into *SEE Political Parties*—Society Engaged Electronic Political Parties. Ironically, it is by giving more power to the people that they will improve their chances of winning and staying in power.

SEE Governments

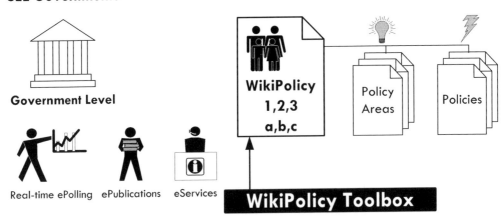

Like modern-day political parties, contemporary governments have become quite comfortable with online technologies. Canada, for instance, offers many **ePublications** and **eServices**. Embracing Wikipolicy at the **Government Level** will only encourage the expansion of the use of online technology, including real-time **ePolling**, which will serve those in power by providing a clear indication of where the people stand on certain important issues.

Traditionally, forming government is every political party's goal. It follows that the Wikipolicy of the governing party becomes that of the democratic jurisdiction (nation, province, state, city, etc.), only now opened up to all SEEtizens, not just members of the party. This is not to say that the Wikipolicy constitutes the law of the land; not at all. Just like party policy today, Wikipolicy constitutes the intentions of the party (and its members) for the jurisdiction moving forward. The difference is, after winning a majority of votes on the basis of its Wikipolicy, the newly formed government opens its intentions for debate to all SEEtizens in the jurisdiction, even those who may have voted against them. This is essential because, after all, party Wikipolicies are open to members only, potentially limiting the scope and nature of debate on certain issues. By transferring a party Wikipolicy into the Wikipolicy of the land, a much more rigorous online debate can take place between proactive SEEtizens intending to make a contribution. This effectively extends the inclusiveness of any democratic process well beyond election campaigns and into day-to-day governance.

At first blush, governments may feel threatened by having open season declared on their policy positions. Upon closer inspection, however, certain advantages to government begin to emerge. For starters, they have a whole new contingent of hearts and minds available to them to debate, decide, and fine-tune policies, taking a great deal of pressure off the exhausting theatrical spectacle of traditional public debate and partisanship. Politicians who monitor eDebates taking place online can voice the specific comments, questions, concerns, and ideas of their constituents rather than constantly trying to come up with their own rejoinders for the sake of argument. Voting purely along party lines would slowly become a thing of the past as politicians in power shift from being dedicated to their party's agenda to being dedicated to their constituents' will and the nation's agenda. Cross partisanship, collaboration, compromise, and partnership will be the order of the day as the emergent and ever-evolving Wikipolicy of the nation affects day-to-day governance. The very nature of politicians' work will change to one of less talk, more action. I don't know of any person who has entered politics with the earnest intention of serving their country and constituents who would not welcome a more dynamic, inclusive, and decisive mechanism for healing divisions and getting things done.

Ultimately, the advantage of Wikipolicy for government is that it forever changes the dynamic of democracy from a traditional, adversarial relationship—governors and the governed—to a more post-modern collaborative relationship—public partners in governance and their elected officials, the stewards and executors of Wikipolicy. Technically speaking, the details will need to be ironed out, but the first generation of Wikipolicy applications will no doubt accomplish that; besides, jurisdictions around the world will also have their own unique take on the technology and intentions of Wikipolicy, in accordance with the collective will of their people—just as the spirit of democracy had originally intended, and as it should be.

Call to Action

SEE Democracy is anything but a pipe dream. You need look no further than the internet to see vibrant communities of political activists, critics, bloggers, etc. If you are an activist, critic, blogger, or member of one of these online communities, wouldn't it make sense to channel the time and energy you put into making your voice heard online into actual policy direction? If you are an elected representative, the leader of a political party (in power or not), or an active member of one, wouldn't you like to be at the forefront of the evolution of democracy? Re-engage a generation of young people, re-energize the political process, and re-tool the huge online community of critics into a community of contributors: this is the short-term promise of SEE Democracy. To learn more, or find out how to get started down the exciting path toward SEE Democracy, visit www.attlas.ca. If you just want to share your thoughts about the whole concept and read what others have to say about it, join the Attlas Project's online social network at www.attlas.org.

Society
Enriching &
Entertaining
Culture

SEE Growth in Personal & Societal Happiness & Development

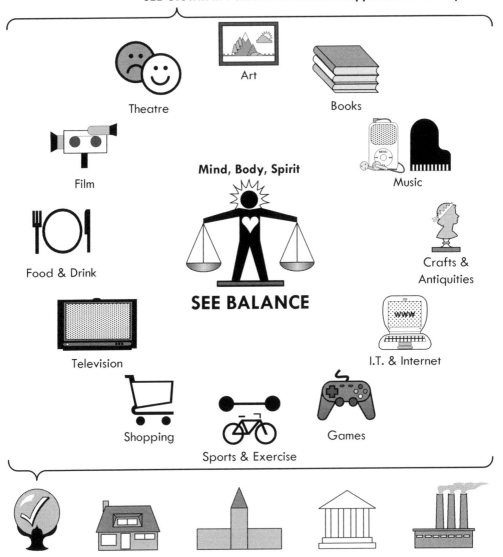

Theatre

Art

Books

Film

Mind, Body, Spirit

Music

Food & Drink

SEE BALANCE

Crafts & Antiquities

Television

I.T. & Internet

Shopping

Games

Sports & Exercise

SEE Long-term Integrity in Community, Institutions, Government & Industry

CHAPTER FOUR
SEE CULTURE

SEE another Definition: SEE Culture

So far, "SEE" has stood for Strategize, Engage, Execute as in SEE VISUAL AID; Social, Environmental, Economic, as in SEE Commerce, SEE Valuation, and SEEconomics; and Society Engaged Electronic Democracy or SEE Democracy. In this, the final case study of Volume one, SEE takes on one more definition: **Society Enriching and Entertaining Culture—SEE Culture.**

What is Culture?

There are probably as many definitions of culture on the books as there have been cultures. According to Wikipedia:

> Culture (from the Latin cultura stemming from colere, meaning "to cultivate") generally refers to patterns of human activity and the symbolic structures that give such activities significance and importance. Cultures can be "understood as systems of symbols and meanings that even their creators contest, that lack fixed boundaries, that are constantly in flux, and that interact and compete with one another."

> Culture can be defined as all the ways of life including arts, beliefs, and institutions of a population that are passed down from generation to generation. Culture has been called "the way of life for an entire society." As such, it includes codes of manners,

dress, language, religion, rituals, games, norms of behaviour such as law and morality, and systems of belief as well as the arts.

Cultural anthropologists most commonly use the term "culture" to refer to the universal human capacity and activities to classify, codify and communicate their experiences materially and symbolically. Scholars have long viewed this capacity as a defining feature of humans (although some primatologists have identified aspects of culture such as learned tool making and use among humankind's closest relatives in the animal kingdom).

Source: http://en.wikipedia.org/wiki/Culture

As an undergraduate some 15 years ago, I studied post-modern linguistics and I recall it being hammered into me that culture and language are indivisible, and that language—as a societal operating system of mobilization and constraint—directly impacts (and is impacted by) culture. Next, consider the assertion discussed in Chapter one that all knowledge exists in one language or another, which means all conscious intelligence is mediated in one form or another (once again, McLuhan's mantra *the medium is the message* rears its iconic head). Taking all of this into account, we end up with a quite complex and detailed definition of culture, with a little chicken-and-egg dilemma to boot. Do humans define culture or are they defined by culture? Which came first? Do we have control over culture? Do we even want to control it? Yes, there's a lot of complexity and detail in a nebulous definition that leaves many questions unanswered. As we know from Chapter one, it's difficult to work with a complex concept from a big picture point of view, so let's conduct a quick mental VISUAL AID process and see if we can arrive at a more simple definition or model of culture with which to work.

Shapes and patterns: of what other system are human beings a part that is in a constant state of flux, has no fixed boundaries, with various elements that appear in competition with one another, defines us, and yet is not beyond our influence and impact? The answer is the natural world—our environment. Just like any other organism, we human beings have a place in the natural world. It contributes to and has an impact on us just as we give back to it and have an impact on it. While in the past, nature was perceived in terms of competition and struggle, I think it safe to say that more enlightened views prevail in our contemporary understanding of nature as a system based more on cooperation, interdependency, and symbiosis. As touched on in the introduction to this book, the obvious difference between an artificial system and the natural world is "intelligent design" (although this is still a heated debate among scientists and theologians). No matter which side of the debate you fall on—whether you believe intelligent design is behind the universe or not—you cannot reasonably deny that a good deal of human design is behind human systems, and that culture is for the most part a series of human systems. So once again, following a VISUAL AID approach produces a biomimetic model for understanding culture that is common to all people at all times throughout the history of humankind. Culture is the environment of humanity that both defines human nature and is defined by human nature in any given society at any given point in time. Simply put, culture is human nature.

Culture as Human Nature

I can hear alarm bells going off in the minds of academics and intellectuals everywhere—from socio-anthropologists and my former linguistics professors to southern Baptist ministers. The term "human nature" tends to be as semantically volatile as any philosophical stick of dynamite you can think of, but bear with me a moment. For starters, my use of the term human nature is a bit of a pun: matching patterns in human phenomena with patterns in nature to reveal a biomimetic model for discussing culture. At the same time it's not a pun at all; I am making the assertion that fundamental human nature does not exist independently or outside of culture, just as no human being can exist independently or outside of nature. How could they?

You cannot come out of a womb without there being one in the first place. If you go back far enough in history, the very first Homo sapiens to be born had to come out of the womb of a creature that was not quite human—a humanlike ancestor who was just another hominid member of the natural world in a series of hominid species. To this day the physical bodies that define us as human are subject to direct physical interaction (and intervention) by our physical environment and the natural world. From genetics to diet and exercise, the size, shape, and health of our bodies depend on a multitude of physical and environmental factors. Consider that astronauts cannot yet survive on the International Space Station without regular supply trips from earth via the Space Shuttle. Even if one day we are able to build a fully self-supporting and self-sustaining space station for humans without such an umbilical cord, that station will have to be a life-giving, life-sustaining environment. No physical being can come into form or maintain its existence without having a more-or-less advantageous relationship with its environment, be it natural or artificial.

In much the same way, the human mind does not exist in a vacuum. No human being comes out of the womb quoting Shakespeare, believing in jihad, hankering for an Angus beef burger, or wanting to wear Prada. Our understanding of the world comes from our experience of both the physical and intellectual environments in which we develop. Cheetahs are not born hunters. They may be born carnivores, but they must learn to hunt from their mother who rears them for at least two years before they are ready to head out on their own. Still, we would say hunting is a part of cheetah nature, wouldn't we? I have had the pleasure of owning two terriers in my lifetime, a Scotty and a Cairn. There is definitely something in their blood that makes them want to hunt and kill small rodents, but it was encouraged if not instilled in them by humans over many centuries of breeding terriers for pest control. What I'm saying is that, from a big-picture perspective of humanity, there is no such thing as nature versus nurture. This is a false dichotomy that denies the fact that nurturing itself is a natural process, and that, at a macro level, an organism's nature (genetics, instinct) is the encoded culmination of generations of nurturing undergone by its species, either by "mother nature" herself, or human intervention by way of domestication and breeding. Every kind of behaviour in all of nature had to be learned at some point, even those we identify as genetic or instinctive behaviours. Behaviour that developed countless generations earlier through trial and error that proved successful to an organism's ability to survive, thrive, and reproduce in the environment encouraged the evolution of physical characteristics in the species as a whole that supported that behaviour. For example, generations of hunter-scavengers relying on scent for survival eventually evolved a heightened sense of smell. Subsequent generations inheriting this crucial physical trait continued and/or intensified the hunter-scavenger behaviour it supported. The results of this evolutionary process can be seen in animals like the grizzly bear and great white shark, both possessing a phenomenal sense of smell, both learning throughout their relatively long lives which scents to pursue and which ones to avoid. Human behaviour—human nature, culture—is likewise a combination of inherent tendencies and predispositions with which we are born intermingling with beliefs and behaviours we pick up during our lifetime from the physical and intellectual influences in our environment.

Just like everything else in nature, culture evolves over time. There is no element of human experience that has remained entirely constant since the first Homo sapiens began scratching out a meagre existence on the planet. Let's consider a few examples. From cave drawings, Egyptian hieroglyphs, Greek mosaics, and medieval frescos to the art of the Renaissance, the development of Impressionism and then Modernism, and the myriad visual art styles that have developed since, it's safe to say that an evolutionary process has been at work. Look at all the diverse branches of Christianity in existence today, despite their being born of a more or less common religious tradition. A similar phenomenon can be seen in other religions to one degree or another. Science and technology have also followed a developmental process, with each new discovery building on the foundations of the day—the new discoveries of the past. Sir Isaac Newton perhaps said it best: "If I have been able to see further than others, it is because I have stood on the shoulders of giants." One way to get a sense of the evolutionary process at work in culture is to examine cultural phenomena that died out. The hippy protest movement of the 60's gave way to the "me" generation of the 70's, and then to Reaganomics and Thatcherism in the 80's. Throughout history, entire cultures and civilizations have more or less vanished from the face of the earth. The study of how a civilization met its end is often as involved as the examination of why a particular species went extinct, and, not surprisingly, often involves similar variables such as foreign invaders and diseases, climate change or other environmental catastrophes, and an inability to adapt quickly enough. As for internal struggles leading to total collapse of a population, my guess is that in earth's 4.5 billion year history, humans are the only species to exhibit such folly.

Human beings are not shy of meddling with the process of evolution in the natural world, and we certainly haven't shied away from full-blown intelligent design when it comes to culture. Ancient rites and rituals had real purpose in the minds of the shaman and priestesses who created them and the participants who enacted them, just as modern-day ceremonies have meaning for contemporary believers. The same can be said for stories and theatre, music and painting, architecture and handicrafts, and the myriad other forms of creative expression of the human condition. On a fundamental level, all aspects of culture must have been invented, designed, or engineered at some point. Just as all art began as cave drawings, so too all types of expressions, traditions, and institutions relating to the human condition begin with an original idea (i.e. fulfilling some real or perceived need) and change over time via countless conscious interventions (i.e. adapting to changing needs). Whether on an individual or group basis, conscious intervention in belief, expression, and behaviour is what it means to have "free will." Even an act as simple as striking back at the person who just struck you indicates a choice. The instinct may be self-defence but the choice to run away might serve that instinct better. No, probably the motivation is vengeance, which is not instinctive at all but rather a belief in the right to retribution based on satiation of the ego. This belief—also known as justice—is cultural. It may be natural and instinctive to feel pain, anger, sadness, fear, etc., but making a counter-attack is not automatic, nor is it without thought. So while we can recognize what we call free will in culture (human nature), "creation" or "intelligent design" is a more problematic concept.

What can human beings think, say, or do in a vacuum? What can we create that is free of any and all cultural influences, histories, physical and/or intellectual paradigms, etc.? The answer is *nothing*. Human beings cannot create in a vacuum anymore than we can exist in one. We procreate, of course, just as all living things do, but we cannot snap our fingers and bring something into being without the fundamental cause-and-effect mechanism of the universe coming into play. We take what we find in our environment—physical or cultural—and manipulate, rearrange, reorganize, re-imagine, and ultimately reproduce it in some altered form. Many New Age traditions maintain that creative thoughts can appear suddenly and spontaneously in our minds, as if this constitutes an act of pure creation from beyond the world of form. Unfortunately, in order for us to be able to register a thought, it must be in a form familiar to our conscious mind: words, music, shapes and patterns, etc. So while it seems as though we can create something from nothing in our minds, what we are in fact doing is expressing accumulated bits and pieces rearranged in new ways, apparently spontaneously and instantaneously. There is no classically defined creation—manifestation of something completely original out of the void—in the human condition. The best we can hope to achieve is better described as *transformation*—taking existing elements and transforming them into something new. In essence, we can say we co-create culture through the interaction between our free will and the natural evolutionary process. This is obviously very similar to how we co-create in the physical and natural worlds. We take stock of what we have to work with (be it technology, biology, knowledge, art, traditions, institutions, etc.), and make desired improvements which, if they "work" and "stick," transform the thing into a "new and improved" version on which future transformations can be based. Being limited to co-creation is nothing to be ashamed of; but, it has been—and continues to be—the root problem behind an epoch of human nature defined by conflict and suffering. The cultural implications of humankind's inability to be godlike—that is, humankind's inability to instantaneously create, control, and/or change the circumstances of reality according to free will—are found throughout history, *a story*, as it were, of *separation*.

A Story of Separation

A Google search on the word "conflict" returns 136 million results—nearly double that of the search term "oxygen." (The term "competition," by the way, returns 214 million results, versus 117 million for "cooperation.") It would be hard to deny that the worldview of the majority of nations and cultures throughout recorded history (certainly among empires both past and present) has been defined by struggle and conflict in one form or another. Greek mythology is for all practical purposes the archetypal blueprint for modern-day soap operas. *Tony Soprano* would have been proud to have any of the scheming, conniving, and murderous gods of ancient Greece on his crew, just as he would no doubt enjoy playing the despotic, all-powerful, and vengeful God of some monotheistic religions. Survey the daily news for yourself and count the number of bad-news stories versus feel-good stories. Why is there such a disproportionate amount of the former? Psychologists might attribute it to a kind of voyeurism: insatiable human curiosity coupled with a desire for experiencing the taboo without having to dirty oneself in the process. Watching horrifying events affecting other people on television or reading about them in the newspaper is a way for individuals to experience those events vicariously and at a safe distance. Journalists are supposed to present news in an objective manner (theoretically at least, Fox News and others notwithstanding), putting the observer in the position of ultimate judge. Faced with the news of a violent street crime, we might choose to take sides with either the victim (someone who "didn't deserve to die") or the accused ("also a victim: of poverty and society's failings"). On yet another level, we may assimilate the knowledge of this latest incident of violence to reinforce an existing belief or worldview we hold (i.e., "the world is a dangerous place full of evil people" or "inner city youths are all violent gang members"). One thing is certain: judging other people and events focuses our ego on external circumstances and keeps our own judgmental eye from inadvertently looking inward at ourselves. But does this really answer the question, why so many bad news stories?

A Cultural Legacy of Bad News Stories

Do you remember being taught the different kinds of stories—their basic plotlines—in grade school? This might refresh your memory:

- *man versus man*
- *man versus nature*
- *man versus God*
- *man versus himself*

Is it just me, or do we see a pattern here? When have you ever read a fictional novel about unconditional love? Not a romance novel, but a tale of pure love? You can pick up a biography of Mother Teresa or Francis of Assisi, perhaps, but you aren't going to find an episode of *Dexter* dedicated to peace and harmony. Now, that is not to say that at the end of the dramatic telling of a conflict there isn't a resolution of said conflict. When one or more of the four basic plotlines reach their climax, traditionally there is some sort of resolution and return to an idealized state of order, if not the establishment of a new order: *and they lived happily ever after,* etc. This brings us closer to answering the question: why so much conflict?

The designation "order" has very little meaning to us without its antithesis "chaos." This is what we call a dichotomy: a pair of opposite concepts whose meanings are essentially dependent on an antithetical relationship with one another; in addition, it is generally accepted by convention that one half of the pair is held in higher regard than the other. We are all familiar with the classic dichotomy of good and evil, for instance. It is fair to say that the concept of good or goodness is held almost universally in higher regard than its counterpart, evil. Other such classic dichotomies include right and wrong, black and white, day and night, and many more. Since one of the two is usually held in higher esteem, and the two are opposites, it follows that one should "rule" the other. Think of mythologies relating to the sun and the moon, as told for instance in the Egyptian myth of Horus and Set. Horus (the sun god, giver of life) and Set (the god of darkness, death, and the underworld) are locked in a never-ending struggle to dominate the earth; however, so long as the sun rises each day, Horus defeats Set and banishes him back into the underworld. This leads us to conclude that our culture of conflict has grown around a nucleus defined by dichotomies. It wasn't until Einstein came along that the concept of relativity challenged the nature of dichotomies like good and evil and right and wrong as fixed truths. Post-modern theory placed one dichotomy behind all others: self and other. Practically speaking, I prefer to think of this post-modern dichotomy as a twin-helix DNA at the core of all human nature, culture, and history: I and you; us and them—self *versus* other.

Man versus Nature

One can see why the dichotomies I/you and us/them dominate our thought process, given that human beings developed self-awareness along an evolutionary process. According to Wikipedia, self-awareness is "the concept that one exists as an individual, separate from other people, with private thoughts." (http://en.wikipedia.org/wiki/Self-awareness). By that definition, scientists have only been able to identify a handful of animals that conclusively possess self-awareness, using a complex series of measures—intelligence, neuron development, awareness, and caring for self and others—culminating in a *mirror test:* animals that are able to recognize their own reflection in a mirror as an image of themselves. Such animals include bottlenose dolphins, all the great apes, killer whales, and elephants (http://en.wikipedia.org/wiki/Mirror_test). In my opinion, the ability to recognize oneself in a mirror seems like an anthropomorphized definition of self-awareness. I see many creatures as having a basic sense of self that allows them—among other things—to identify themselves in relationship to potential predators, competitors, mates, and prey. Dogs can recognize their own scent, no mirror required. And, I might add, my dog certainly knows what he wants, independent of what everyone else in "the pack" may want; at the same time, he knows to guard the pack's territory (our home) against intruders with his life if need be. Whether directly linked to self-awareness or not, the dichotomy of I/us and you/them appears to be completely natural.

Where human beings begin to move beyond what is commonplace elsewhere in the natural world is in assessment of that which we perceive and experience in nature. Basic observations of the average mammal living in the wild reveal a life that most of us would describe as a constant struggle for survival. It's hard to know what exactly goes on in an animal's mind, and while the basic thought, "I must survive," is not beyond the realm of possibility even for a small rodent, the thought, "running for my life sucks big time, I wish I were a hawk or grizzly bear instead," is probably beyond the scope of our furry mammalian cousins. Our tendency to look upon life as a struggle for survival is reflected in the predominant predator-versus-prey theme found in so many nature documentaries. Not surprisingly, then, we have often defined our own existence as a struggle for survival, and as a species we developed a psychological need to overcome and dominate the environment, emphasizing our position at the top of the food chain. This confirmed our status as creatures of the highest order on earth—a rare commonality between evolutionary and religious schools of thought. Judgment of life's predicaments and one's relative place in the order of things is beyond self-awareness; it is *self-consciousness:* an individual's understanding of their own identity and/or place in the world, also called *the ego.* Somewhere along the line, human beings moved beyond simple self-awareness to self-consciousness or self-referential awareness. Our species began not only to experience (as all creatures do) and be aware that those experiences are unique to us as individuals (as some higher order creatures do) but to think about, share thoughts about, even record those experiences. We began to question our very existence and then reason and imagine explanations to make sense of it all. This was the birth of culture: an intellectual schism that meant we would never again see ourselves as "just another part of nature."

Homo sapiens weren't the only hominids to have used tools in prehistoric times, just as we are not the only creatures alive today to use them. The study of great ape society and behaviour in the 20th century has shown their capacity for cognition and empathy in far more impressive ways than initially imagined. Intellectually what truly sets human beings apart from other creatures is the need to expand understanding of our experience of the natural world. Early cave drawings show images of animals, people, and what look like hunting parties. Hunting animals for food and skins was an essential aspect of early humans' survival. But why, around 30,000 years ago, did making a pictorial record of the hunt become a matter of significance? Were they trying to communicate with one another, reviewing their last hunt, and/or planning a strategy for the next hunt? Was there a shaman among them who used cave painting as a way of deifying their activities to appease the gods? Was it as simple as creating a visual aid to help recount the tale of the hunt for those who were not present for the violent and potentially dangerous affair? Or was it simply a doodle, a work of prehistoric graffiti? Whatever the rationale, one thing is certain: no other creature in nature could *create* as humans did. Creativity defined for us a higher order of being, and we praised the highest order of being, our *Creator*—God, Allah, the Great Mother, the Grand Architect, et al. Our self-consciousness and creativity reinforced our ego: we forged ever more deadly weapons and hunting strategies, our shamans came up with ever more powerful rights and rituals to effect change in the world, our artisans and engineers crafted ever more beautiful and functional vessels and buildings. In short, we began to identify less with nature and more with the gods (i.e., *God created man in His own image*, and *as above, so below*).

If there's one thing about the ego, it's that it doesn't really like being number two. The first dichotomy that human beings developed in the us versus them category was man versus nature. Because early human's perception was one of struggling to survive in a harsh natural environment (a perception that changed very little through the millennia), and the ego didn't like being number two, it was obvious who would come out on top in any contest. The ego, quite naturally, is all about self-preservation, self-gratification, self-stratification, self, self, self. You can see ego at work in males competing for alpha status in their group. So it is natural for Homo sapiens to have developed a culture that established itself as the alpha species in the world. We became the judge of what constituted order and chaos in the natural kingdom and behaved accordingly. When it became second-nature for humans to hunt with weapons, store food and water in vessels, plant crops, breed livestock, change entire landscapes, etc., culture had come into its own, one step above nature, and we were its masters. It's no wonder tales of man versus nature have always been popular. No matter what beast stepped out of line to challenge humankind's supremacy, ultimately the latter would win. Humans were at the top of the food chain, we were the masters of the plant and animal kingdoms, and sooner or later we would always prevail. The pesky dandelion would be weeded out of the garden, the rogue beast would be tamed, caged, or killed, and all would be well in the world once more in our eyes. There was only one little catch: *acts of God*.

Man versus God

If you read something as mundane and practical as your life or home insurance policy, you will likely come across a clause in it that cites "acts of God." Since the dawn of civilization, people have seen frightening, destructive, and generally inexplicable natural events as acts of God (the will of the gods, the wrath of God, etc.). Cataclysms befalling humankind indicated angry and vengeful deities determined to punish and impugn mere mortals for breaking their divine laws or otherwise angering them. So-called "miraculous" events were taken for granted, and it was an absence of plague, drought, and other catastrophes that indicated the gods were happy with the state of the world and humankind in general. To this day, natural disasters like floods, tornadoes, lightning strikes, hurricanes, earthquakes, etc. are referred to as acts of God in insurance jargon—natural disasters, the cause of which cannot be attributed any blame. Of course, in the ancient world, blame was attributed—and often. Humans have a long history of sacrificing flora, fauna, friend, and foe alike to appease their deities. For ancient peoples, the stories of the gods were not allegorical tales; they were imaginations serving as literal explanations for phenomena of which they could otherwise make no sense, such as their own existence and the true nature of the universe. The anthropomorphized nature of many early deities and mythologies was simply a projection of known human experience upon the world of the unknown, with an "as above, so below" logic. The problem—at least for the ego—was that no matter how much effort mystics put into making the gods susceptible to the same passions, vices, and natural laws as mankind, the fact remained that Zeus could hurl thunderbolts from atop Mount Olympus. Let's face it, for an ego that believes it is a being of a higher order at the top of all creation, being zapped by lightning, covered by ash and lava, or swallowed by an earthquake is a bruising reality check. On a more mundane level, the gods were immortal; men and their egos were anything but.

Why would the Creator treat its most incredible creation—us—with such impunity? This question has baffled theologians and philosophers for millennia. The Christian concept of original sin as told in the story of Adam and Eve and the expulsion from the Garden of Eden is one classic explanation. The Devil, disguised as a serpent, tells Eve and Adam to bite of the Fruit of Knowledge and they will become godlike. This doesn't go over very well with God, who explicitly told them not to eat that fruit, and so Adam and Eve are banished from Eden into a "fallen world" where they will be slaves to their passions and engage in a constant struggle not only for survival, but for the fate of their immortal souls. A major goal of human beings, not only from a Judeo-Christian perspective but from that of other world religions, is to worship God (Allah, Krishna, etc.) and seek redemption—reach the Promised Land, Heaven, Nirvana, etc. As a direct result of the ego, an almost universal aspect of culture has been to try and make sense of humankind's position at the top of the natural world while at the same time being subject to the whims of a Creator who clearly demonstrates the power of divine intervention and the will to use it.

Caveats

Many cultures throughout history have taken a less confrontational view of their relationship with the world, both in terms of man versus nature and man versus God. Of note are the many aboriginal peoples who saw themselves at one with nature; and, rather than anthropomorphizing an image of God that was somehow separate from themselves and the world, they deified nature itself, believing that all things—animals, plants, even the rocks and the clouds—contained the essence of the Great Spirit within them. It wasn't that indigenous peoples who lived off the land didn't see themselves as unique individuals within nature; they recognized a duality to existence. In a bear they saw both the bear's body and the bear spirit. Certain animal spirits embodied particular attributes such as strength, agility, cunning, etc., which the people recognized within themselves as well. They would ask the animal spirits to grant them greater power in those attributes. Rites of passage into manhood often included elaborate trials, tests, and ceremonies, sometimes culminating in the appearance and/or hunting of a totem animal which would determine what spirit would watch over and guide the young man throughout his life-long journey. An equivalent Christian concept might be the idea of a guardian angel. So while we can identify cultures whose stories have been less about man versus nature and man versus God, there are still two more manifestations of the I/us and you/them dichotomy to consider.

Man versus Man

Even aboriginal cultures who sought to be one with both the natural world and the spirit world could not escape the world of man versus man—the culture of conflict. Here is an absolute, undeniable, and universal narrative expression of I/us and you/them. No culture, past or present, has been completely free of conflict between two or more individuals or groups. It seems to be a universal constant in human nature; and, far from being taboo, it has been for the most part heralded, glorified, encouraged, and celebrated. *Why?* The stock answer includes the struggle for survival, scarcity of resources, etc., but surely the real reason is because of the related dichotomy of victory and defeat. One may or may not relish a victory over nature, but the ego boost and poetic significance of victory in a *mano e mano* contest is inarguable. Firefighters battling wildfires in Southern California do not return from the front lines of their struggle against the forces of nature (or acts of God) as decorated heroes; at least, not in the same way that soldiers returning from war do, or athletes returning from the Olympics. We have no day dedicated to "veterans of natural disasters." We don't necessarily have to think about human conflict in terms of war between nations or even tribal disputes; petty squabbles between neighbours or family members also constitute conflict between people. And as far as encouragement and glorification go, competition is not only promoted, it is rewarded in sports, academics, politics, business, and just about all areas of our lives. Yes, competition and conflict between humans appears to be a universal constant in culture.

Human beings have a long history of designing and engineering conflict for all sorts of reasons. From the Greeks who held the first Olympics for the sake of glory during times of relative peace, to the Romans who threw slaves into the Coliseum to slaughter one another for the entertainment of the masses, to wars of convenience began by covert means for the economic benefit of one or more participating nation, the value human beings have placed on putting one another to the test has been a constant throughout history. To answer the question *why,* one need only turn to the concept of victory again. *To the victor go the spoils.* Here we see the link between competition, materialism, and consumption. But victory isn't limited to material gain, it also provides self-conscious gratification. Primates competing for alpha male status stand to gain first pick of just about everything in the tribe, from females to food, but in addition to the material benefits of winning, comes a self-gratifying sense of power, authority, control, superiority, etc. Victory feeds the body and the ego. It is the insatiable ego—a completely natural aspect of self-awareness common throughout nature—that appears to drive evolutionary development in many species, particularly where a strong hierarchical group dynamic exists, especially among omnivorous and carnivorous mammals living in groups, packs, or prides. The primal rush and ego gratification that comes from engaging in conflict with members of one's own species appears to be an inherent mechanism of evolution that encourages individuals to compete with each other in order to ensure a more resilient gene pool over time. Survival of the fittest calls for constant tests of fitness.

This basic approach has also been applied to every aspect of contemporary human life, particularly free market capitalism. Competition and the right to survive—or go bankrupt—are best left to "natural forces" at work in the marketplace. At the time of this writing, Barack Obama's administration is negotiating additional aid for General Motors and Chrysler on top of the some $17 billion in bailouts they received from George W. Bush. Clearly, some behemoths of industry are too important to the overall economic environment to be allowed to just go extinct; much to the dismay of the outgoing U.S. President who seemed to indicate his preference would be to let nature take its course. In academia, too, ideas have come into being and gone the way of the dodo. I am not making an argument for *Social Darwinism*, a theory that I consider to be erroneous and not in the same ballpark as the biomimetic model of culture I am proposing here. That said, I cannot deny that elitist elements have used evolutionary biology, paleoanthropology, and cultural studies to promote all sorts of racist theories and pseudo-science, including eugenics (a great read on this subject is Stephen J. Gould's *The Mismeasure of Man*). Again, the ego doesn't like to be number two, and it will go to great lengths, using all its available faculties, to compete for (and/or convince itself that it already occupies) the number-one spot.

Man versus Himself

The problem with being number one for the ego, not surprisingly, is that it can't be there forever. There are two sides to every conflict between human beings, and invariably both sides believe they are right (righteous, have the right to victory and the spoils, etc.). There is always a loser in the win-loss scenario, and while today an individual may be the winner—his ego gratified, his hierarchical status established and secured—tomorrow he may be the loser, his ego shattered, his hierarchical status reduced or taken away. Of course, the longer an individual sits at the top of the game, the greater the likelihood that fear and anxiety will set in. Our ego is a product of self-consciousness; therefore, just as surely as ego is the first to pat itself on the back soon after a victory, it is also the first to become neurotic over the thought of losing. Ego is all too pragmatic about these things: it knows nothing lasts forever, but that doesn't stop it from creating all kinds of self-delusions to keep the party going, so to speak, for as long as possible. The very element of consciousness that drives individuals to win inadvertently sets itself up for eventual failure and disappointment. What is this if not a conflict with oneself?

There is another problem altogether with winning, especially when it comes to man-versus-man conflicts. Being right in an argument, stealing from someone, defeating one's opponent, killing an enemy, conquering a nation, hoarding a disproportionate amount of resources while others live in scarcity, etc., all come at the expense of another individual or group. This, at least for some, is cause for an entirely different internal conflict—a *conflict of conscience*. A struggle with one's own conscience may seem personal but is as affected and influenced by culture as the ego's struggle with winning and losing (that is, being seen as a "winner" or a "loser"). A conflict of conscience doesn't exist in a vacuum any more than the ego, or any other aspect of human nature. An individual may have been raised to value all life and all living things, and then be faced with the terrible choice of having to take a life to defend a loved one. This is one of those classic philosophical conundrums that can easily eat into hours of conversation time in a coffee shop. Basically, your ego is in tune with what *it wants*, your conscience is in tune with *what is right*. Herein is another fundamental dichotomy in human nature. Just as man versus man leads to the dichotomy of victory and defeat, man versus himself is all about the dichotomy of right and wrong.

The problem from a philosophical—even metaphysical—perspective is: just what is "right" and what is "wrong"? The whole question of morality comes into play here, as do concepts like etiquette, decency, religiosity, etc., all of which have been heady subjects at the heart of culture for millennia. There are no easy answers, and the volumes written on the subject, from psychology manuals to civil-rights speeches to religious texts, defies summation. However, I think it is generally accepted in the modern world that the only reasonable definition of morality we can hope to agree on for the time being (at least here in the West) goes something like this: *you can do whatever is "right" for you in your life, so long as doing so does not interfere with what is "right" for someone else and their life*. Regardless of whether you agree with this definition of morality or not, you still have a moral sense that has no doubt been put to the test at one time or another in your life. On occasion, your morals—learned values and beliefs coupled with an instinctive knowing about what is right and wrong—fail to give you clear guidance when faced with some moral dilemma. You end up feeling split between two opposing viewpoints within your own consciousness—*a mind at war with itself*.

Ego consciousness is truly a product of nature. Like any sentient life form, the ego needs to feed in order to survive. Ego thrives on all sorts of stimulation, satiation, gratification, recognition, and other external sources to produce and preserve a sense of self. Generally speaking, the ego will not want to put itself at risk or challenge its sense of self, and it will actively seek ways to experience things vicariously through others—risk free. Eventually, these experiences no longer satisfy, and the ego must experience more (in quantity, intensity, etc.) to satisfy its hunger—feed the need. At some point the ego will likely cross the line between vicarious and direct experience, assuming greater amounts of risk in order to satiate itself. Such self-destructive cycles can happen with everything, from food and alcohol, to sex and violence, to sports and gaming. We call it addiction, and psychologists categorize it as a kind of *self-loathing*. The ego is addicted (attached) to a sense of self fed entirely by external experiences that conflict with its own self-preservation instinct.

What about art? Where does it fit in? Surely art is not about conflict. Well, actually, if you read many artists' biographies or talk to contemporary artisans, you will discover that indeed, art is about conflict, struggle, pain, fear, etc. It's practically the ultimate example of man versus himself, and it comes back to the neurosis humans feel for not being God. An artist can paint a flower (or photograph it, write a poem/song about it, etc.), but can never actually make a flower (growing one from a seed doesn't count in this instance). An artist can only go so far in terms of "capturing" or "creating" the beauty, truth, experience, feeling, etc., and this can make him or her quite self-conscious. If artists were capable of creating "perfection," we would have no  need of art critics. Have you ever wondered why it is that some art is acknowledged as being "great" while most art, well, isn't? What about artists who get paid millions for work they personally loathe, but find they cannot make a dime selling their true labour of love? So much has been written on the nature of art and the plight of the artist, that I must admit it would be impossible for me to do justice to the question here. If it's hard for you to think about art in terms of conflict and personal struggle, consider Edvard Munch's *The Scream,* and these lyrics from the song *The Fly:*

> *"Every artist is a cannibal, every poet is a thief, all kill their inspiration and sing about their grief."*

> \- U2

Resolving the Conflict

You will recall that earlier we posed the question, why so many "bad news" stories? It has taken what might seem like a lengthy explanation to come full circle, but given the innumerable volumes written on the subject of human culture, what I've offered here cannot even qualify as a summary. The point was to show that what appears to be a culture of conflict, competition, materialism, and consumption—a human nature defined by struggle—evolved naturally, as did the four classically-defined "human stories." All of it comes down to how we see the world in dichotomies; specifically, the fundamental dichotomy of self and other that is the hallmark of the ego—self-awareness and self-consciousness. We immerse ourselves in stories of conflict—dramas—precisely because they are primal, familiar, and make us feel alive. Is it by accident that we use the same word—*climax*—to describe both the crescendo of a story and the act of sex? And what happens afterward? *Resolution:* a temporary sense of peace and tranquility; a return to normality; a self-gratified ego enjoying the spoils of victory. I recall an expression shared with me in a wine cellar in Europe once: "Do you know why we argue so much? So we can toast making up!" There is an undeniable ego satisfaction that comes from winning an argument, scoring the overtime goal, dating an attractive partner, "kicking an opponent's ass" on Xbox, finishing at the top of the class, scoring the highest sales figures in the office, finally buying that luxury car after years of working your way up the corporate ladder, watching a convicted felon being sentenced in court, witnessing horrendous events affecting others on TV, defeating an opponent in a political contest, and so on. But is it all natural?

The litmus test, then, is to find other examples in nature that support or dispute the assumption. Based on this discussion, I appear to be supporting a biomimetic model of culture, suggesting that it evolved naturally over time, with the caveat that human beings actively meddled in, designed, and engineered systems and elements of it throughout history. I used examples from the animal kingdom that clearly show ego-based conflict as an essential evolutionary mechanism by which organisms grow stronger over time, and by which human beings evolved into the dominant mammalian species on the planet. It seems only logical that the legacy of conflict and competition experienced in the natural world by hominids eventually came to define our physical and intellectual environment—human nature and culture. Based on this, it would appear that our culture of conflict is completely natural, but in fact, our analysis has been shallow and grossly incomplete. In looking at the human narrative, we've seen only one side of the story, and missed an essential force at work in all nature and evolution itself. We have lost sight of the bigger picture. We have lost sight of *love*.

The Culture of Conflict Evolved

What a mother feels for a newborn child is unlike any other bond or connection she may have. The impetus for the dichotomy us and them is based in a sense of connection—and commitment—to the group and its continued survival. Poets and veterans of war have throughout history described the bonds of love and friendship formed between comrades even amid the horrors of war. We human beings hold altruism and self-sacrifice in the highest regard. We may follow leaders, honour authority figures, admire billionaires, and be in awe of famous celebrities, but we venerate saints—individuals who chose to put others' lives before their own. Can this be called self-consciousness? Here we begin to move beyond the left brain's analytical and superficial man-versus-universe view of the natural world, history, and our place in it. Our minds are opened to the bigger picture of the universe, its evolution, and our own—the evolution of love.

There is an unseen, immeasurable, and yet ever-present constant force at work in the universe that has been as common to all cultures as conflict. It has been called many things by many people, including universal consciousness, the God-force, life-force, the law of attraction, but simply put, it is love. If love is everywhere and in everything, then the culture of conflict has love behind it as well. At first blush this may seem hard to swallow: after all, in our minds we see a dichotomy between "love" and "hate," and more often than not, conflict seems to be an act of hate rather than love. In the observable universe in which dichotomies exist, love and hate are relative terms, and the so-called love of one's security, property, family, tribe, monarch, country, and God has been cited time and again as reason enough to hate. How can this be? The answer is simple: it's all love, and it's all perfect. This is not an empty New Age assertion or flippant homage to an old Beatles tune. It's simply a logical argument for explaining how the force behind the observable universe is constantly emerging—evolving— through the unfolding of that universe toward a more perfect manifestation of itself: a more perfect form of love, one that is *transforming*. We as human beings are able to recognize the transformational process of love when we see it, because we all participate in it to one degree or another. The differences between the forms of love with which we are familiar are related to the state of consciousness we have achieved, as shown in the VISUAL AID, below.

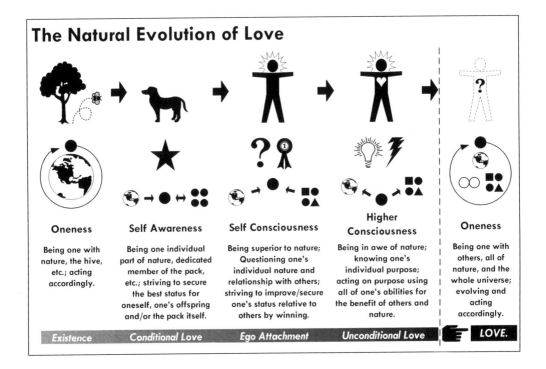

The Natural Evolution of Love

Oneness	Self Awareness	Self Consciousness	Higher Consciousness	Oneness
Being one with nature, the hive, etc.; acting accordingly.	Being one individual part of nature, dedicated member of the pack, etc.; striving to secure the best status for oneself, one's offspring and/or the pack itself.	Being superior to nature; Questioning one's individual nature and relationship with others; striving to improve/secure one's status relative to others by winning.	Being in awe of nature; knowing one's individual purpose; acting on purpose using all of one's abilities for the benefit of others and nature.	Being one with others, all of nature, and the whole universe; evolving and acting accordingly.

Existence	Conditional Love	Ego Attachment	Unconditional Love	LOVE.

The love continuum begins with simple **existence**—the transformational power of love brings a being from the world of formlessness into the world of form. This being is one with nature and the natural world, but it doesn't know it. There is no consciousness, so love (beauty, gratitude) cannot express itself other than through simple existence. Beings at this level of love just exist. There's nothing wrong with that, of course—think of the flowers and the bees that together fill the world with much beauty and nourishing fruit.

The next major leap forward along the continuum, **conditional love**, is linked to self-awareness. The love of a mother for her offspring (which may seem unconditional in that she may be willing to sacrifice herself for her young) is in fact conditional love because she likely would not sacrifice herself for another being. This expression of love serves the self, the family, the group (pack), and the evolutionary process itself very well; it drives the visible struggles and conflicts between competing species and members within societies.

At the next level, self-consciousness, it is not surprising that love is expressed as **ego attachment**: the love of a broader scope of externalities as they define the ego's sense of self—appearance, position, wealth, property, reputation, nationality, religion, etc. Similarly, romantic love—including the concept of loving one person above all others and holding that individual to a "bond" of matrimony—is ego attachment, directly linked to self-consciousness. In ego attachment we define ourselves by what we look like, what we do, whether we are single or married, how much money we earn, to what nation or nationality we belong, and many other external factors derived from our physical and intellectual environments. Not only that, we tend to judge, value, admire, and even "love" others based on these externalities. Ego attachment is a more complex form of conditional love, in that it includes a more highly-evolved ego in the equation, a more complex version of "what's in it for me?" There is give-and-take at work at this level of love, and the ego seeks either a fair exchange, or to come out ahead. Ironically, this apparently self-centred expression of love actually represents advancement over conditional love.

Unconditional love is achieved when people think, feel, and act from a state of higher consciousness, an inner knowing that the dichotomy I/you and us/them is an illusion, just as nature versus nurture makes sense only until you step back and consider the bigger picture. From a broad enough perspective and long enough timeline, one begins to see the emergent nature of the universe as a complete system driven by love's intention to know itself in its totality. That is why unconditional love, when it is awakened within an individual, causes them to focus their attention on awe and gratitude for their environment (natural and cultural) and on giving as much of themselves as possible to benefit others. Unconditional love represents a shift in consciousness—in being—toward oneness with others, the planet, and the universe. Individuals who have exhibited higher consciousness in life have described "enlightenment"—as it is often called—as awakening from a dream, dying and being reborn, or going through a gate. Unconditional love and enlightenment tend to be associated with the concepts of spirit, the eternal soul, life after death, etc., all of which have held a prominent place in many cultures around the world. In modern times, evidence for the existence of a soul has been corroborated by a handful of people who have had so-called near-death experiences. New Age traditions have associated spirit and higher consciousness with areas of scientific study ranging from psychology to quantum mechanics. One thing is certain: just like philosophers, artists, and poets through the ages, science has yet to measure, contain, or begin to quantify love.

I contend that the ultimate power of love is *transformation*. As lower levels of consciousness give way to higher, the force of love itself is transformed along the continuum toward its full potential. Love gains in energy, and, at each stage along the transformation process, the power available to the individual being is proportionately increased. This is why so many self-help gurus and New Age thinkers promote the concept of *self actualization* through self-love. Countless programs like *The Secret* promote a combination of "feeling good" (gratitude, positive thinking, laughter, etc.) with positive visualization as a way of being able to channel positive energies to attract positive results into one's life—such as abundance, love, etc. Whether you believe in such claims or not is irrelevant. Love, like gravity, is an observable force in the world of human culture. And, like gravity, love is a force that doesn't differentiate. Gravity, for instance, does not discriminate between an aid package and a bomb—both will fall to earth. Now think of love in the same way—consider passion, for instance. One can begin to understand how love can be behind conflict. Coming back to the discussion of art, it's clear that for a great many artists, the fires of passion fuel their internal struggles as well as their external works. On another level, we're all familiar with *crimes of passion*; Hollywood and the publishing industry have made a fortune based on the concept that passion and violence go hand in hand. Love is a universal force radiating in the world through our lives, reflecting our choices, and revealing our consciousness. In this way, love is a lot like white light: unseen to the eye, yet it reveals the "true colours" of our physical existence.

A Culture of Love?

The path to seeing, feeling, and harnessing the power of love has become one of the fundamental quests of humanity. Not surprisingly, our quest for understanding and communing with love has been the subject of countless stories, poems, songs, paintings, art, crafts, and expressions of every conceivable kind. And yet, for the most part, real love eludes us. The fact that we have been unable to find a universal formula for finding love has been the cause of much anxiety, suffering, and conflict, both literal and literary. Can we ever hope to truly understand the enigma, the ultimate mystery that is love? Many spiritual traditions—both ancient, and newly-rehashed and packaged—will tell you: "Absolutely; it all depends on you." When you see and feel love all around you, you experience its power to reveal and transform yourself and your life. At least, that's what most religions and New Age gurus peddle these days: "here's what's in it for you!" But is the focus on the self—self-redemption, self-actualization, self-empowerment, self-immortality, self, self, self—really the stuff of higher consciousness? As we have seen throughout this chapter, as soon as there's a "self," there must also be an "other." But unconditional love doesn't differentiate; higher consciousness seeks oneness. To truly be in a state of love, there is no I/you; us/them. If love is at the root of human desire, and our attraction to love is ultimately self-serving, then it should come as no surprise that most of us have an ego attachment to the concept of love itself. Most of us were brought up in a culture in which love is a "thing." It can be found and lost. It can sweep us off our feet and also fade away. Love is an object of our desire, the source of much suffering, something to find, seize, and keep. We may say "money can't buy love," but we live as though we believe otherwise.

Where, then, does all this leave the question of culture, and the culture of conflict and consumerism we identified in the first half of this chapter? It's as simple as this: there is no right or wrong when it comes to culture any more than there is any right or wrong in nature; because as we have seen, love is behind all of nature, including human nature—our stories, beliefs, etc. That said, clearly there are experiences of lower consciousness and higher consciousness, just as there are observable, discernable expressions of love. Some of these expressions are more empowering than others. For instance, ego attachment can be the cause of much anxiety—the ego that wins today may fear losing tomorrow; the ego that is attached to the world of form may fear the unknown world of the formless. Since culture has evolved along with consciousness and love, and we can recognize higher consciousness—unconditional love—when we see it (more precisely, when we experience it), it stands to reason that human nature is on an upward evolutionary track. So while we all want to enjoy our journey, we should probably stop and ask ourselves one simple question: is our culture empowering us—our evolution toward a higher state of consciousness—or holding us back? Is indulging in human nature really just a personal choice, or are we missing the bigger picture? Do our thoughts and beliefs about the world and the experiences we pursue promote reaching higher levels of consciousness or do they perpetuate lower levels of being?

SEE Culture – Society Enriching & Entertaining Culture

SEE Culture strikes a balance between indulging all manner of appetites (entertaining our ego) and enriching our lives (developing a sense of oneness with a "self" much greater than our ego). There is no tried-and-true formula for imbuing culture with a sense of unconditional love, but you know it when you encounter it. Whether in print, music, film, television, video games, or a myriad other examples, we each have an inner barometer that lets us know the level of consciousness we are experiencing through participation in any cultural phenomenon. For instance, while I cannot judge the personal passion and integrity of the designers, artists, and programmers of violent video games, I can say without hesitation that most of the "mature" game titles available do little or nothing to promote higher levels of consciousness. As with pornography, alcohol, and drugs, over-consumption of graphic violence is potentially addictive. The rush induced by the frenetic pace, visceral experience, and over-the-top sense of power and control can consume an individual, particularly if their sense of self is fragile. In mid-October 2008, a young boy named Brandon Crisp ran away from home in Barrie, Ontario, after his parents confiscated his Xbox—they felt his addiction to *Call of Duty 4: Modern Warfare* was affecting his grades and his social life. After a three-week search, young Brandon's body was found in the woods near his home. More recently, seventeen-year-old Ohio teen Daniel Petric was convicted of aggravated murder and other charges after shooting his parents for taking away his copy of *Halo 3*. These may be extreme cases, but having played both games briefly myself—I personally found *Call of Duty 4* very unnerving—I can see how neither would do much to reinforce a loving self-image in a teenager. The games not only offer the ego a fantasy world in which it can be dominant and in control, the online achievements, ladders, and tournaments offer the ego a reason to play obsessively in pursuit of national and international recognition in the "real world" of competitive gaming. A mature individual might like the game's realism, challenge, or action and have no particular ego attachment to it. Brandon and Daniel, it seems, developed a dependency on the virtual self-image the game provided them (addiction is a kind of self-loathing), so when the only likeable self-image they had—that of "hardcore gamer"—was taken away from them in an act of conditional love, how else would anyone expect them to react?

Like many people, I grew up playing video games and kept playing them well into adulthood, but never had access to virtual experiences that were as ultra-realistic (not to mention as ultra-violent) as children do today. Growing up, the violence I experienced in games was more cartoonish than anything else; I don't ever recall being thrilled because a game had lots of blood in it, but I had friends who did think blood in games was a measure of "cool"—and that sentiment certainly took hold in the industry. I was in high school when *Mortal Kombat* made waves in the popular media for its "realism" and ultra-violent content (read: lots of blood). I watched the events around various school shootings and listened intently to the heated debates over video game violence:

"do violent video games promote violent behaviour?" I certainly never had the urge to arm myself and express my anger and frustration in the real world, and I played plenty of *Mortal Kombat, Doom, Quake, Diablo,* and many other games. If anything, video games were a way for me to escape from any frustrations I had that day. Mind you, it was always clear to me that it was just a game. I suppose the lack of photo-realism meant that, even subconsciously, it was difficult to lose myself completely in a game, although that's not to say I haven't experienced meditative or semi-hypnotic states while playing (not unlike a runner who enters "the zone"). So despite having played a few games compulsively in the past—most gamers will admit to having been addicted to one game or another—at no point did I ever begin to define a self-image around a virtual experience. The death of Brandon Crisp and the murder of Daniel Petric's mother will, I hope, shift the question away from the side-issue of video-game violence and focus on the heart of the matter: what do video games do for one's self esteem (self love)? And *can* video games promote higher levels of consciousness?

Allow me to be clear on this point: I am not singling out video games. Let's consider another cultural phenomenon on the opposite end of the spectrum that begs the question concerning self-esteem and self love: fashion magazines, particularly those targeted at young girls. Here is an area I must admit I know little about, except that I would, on occasion, browse the analogous men's versions of such magazines—*GQ, Men's Journal,* etc. Again, simply based on my own experience, I can see how glamour magazines do little to promote higher levels of consciousness. The linear cause-and-effect pitch being made is at the level of self awareness: *if* you look like this, *then* you will be beautiful (i.e., lovable). The implications are felt deeply on the level of self-consciousness: if you don't look like this, you are unlovable. There is a similar pitch for men, too, adding: drive this, smell like that, make so much money, and you will be a success (read: you will be lovable and you will have a reason to love yourself). From advertising and media to arts and entertainment and institutions and traditions, culture impacts individuals on a personal as well as society-wide level;

asking if an element within our culture promotes higher levels of consciousness or not is a no-brainer.

Self-consciousness and ego attachment define and dominate mainstream culture today. We are surrounded by—some would say inundated with—messages reinforcing our ego-identification. Look like this; live like that; protect yourself, your family, and your property; win at any cost—these are just a handful of the ego-centric messages of our competitive, consumption-based culture. So what is the answer, then? Are we to turn to some puritanical definition of what is morally appropriate and what isn't? No, a knee-jerk reaction is not the answer. What happens to freedom of expression, freedom of religion, and freedom in general? Nothing; they remain intact. Can we have our cake and eat it too? Yes: we just need to **SEE Balance.**

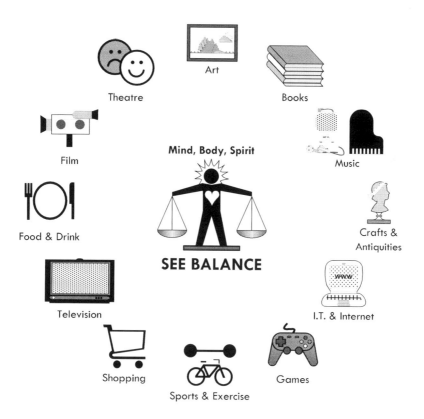

No matter where you look these days, you're likely to encounter the message of living in balance. The mainstream media is becoming more saturated with messages about living a more balanced lifestyle in terms of diet and exercise, stress and relaxation, work and recreation, enterprise and environmentalism, even socializing and solitude. Call it the influence of the New Age movement if you must, but from medicine to Wall Street, it's clear that the West is waking up to the idea that striking the right balance—in mind, body, and spirit—is key to a life of health, happiness, and prosperity. Implicit in the mainstream media's message of balance is the force of love and the potential for higher consciousness. I say "implicit," because for the most part, mainstream messages promoting a balanced lifestyle come pre-packaged with some product or service. The concepts of unconditional love and higher consciousness are seen by many to belong to the realm of spirituality or religion; they carry too much baggage about saints and self-sacrifice, and they simply don't mesh with a culture based on self-interest and material advancement (competition and consumerism). Even some so-called New Age messages have focused on selling self-love for its self-help and personal power effects, leaving higher consciousness and unconditional love out of the picture. In terms of awakening to higher consciousness, mainstream culture is still pretty groggy, with one eye half-open, at best. It's no surprise that its messages of balance are mostly subjective, isolated, and incomplete. To put it bluntly, our culture is still out of balance, but it's nothing to be ashamed of: it is simply going through a completely natural process of evolution. We all must walk before we can run; we must wallow in the murk of our own self-absorption before we can break free and break through to higher ground. You can see it happening all around you; maybe inside you, too.

Remember, everything in nature evolved from lower life forms but none is "right" or "wrong." We have all seen films that are violent—some even ultra-violent—and yet promote a higher sense of understanding, appreciation, beauty, love, etc. There is nothing wrong with promoting beauty, if it promotes positive self-image. Proctor and Gamble promotes an advertising campaign for a type of soap that shows ordinary women instead of supermodels—it's a step in the right direction. There's nothing wrong with wanting to indulge an intrinsic and natural aspect of our humanity—sexuality, for instance—while recognizing that sex can be a gateway to higher consciousness, and can transform a physical act into a blissful experience that goes far beyond any sensory stimulation or ego-gratification. As for fantasy and science fiction, it is not by accident that series like *Star Wars* and *Star Trek* have proven so popular (any film critic will tell you it has nothing to do with good writing or acting). Consider *Star Wars:* for all its entertaining special effects, swashbuckling action, and classic good-versus-evil themes, it touched upon a deep knowing inside us all: that *the force* has a *light side* and a *dark side,* and it's up to us to bring *balance* to the universe. With a very different approach, *Star Trek* touches on another deep longing inside us all as a species: to get our collective act together, put aside our petty differences, inherit our birthright, and *boldly go where no one has gone before.* Even with conflict-filled stories, *Star Trek* struck the right balance between visceral action-adventure, intellectual stimulation, and hope for an enlightened future filled with infinite possibility.

So long as our culture is on the path to achieving the right balance of mind, body, and spirit, *entertaining and enriching society,* it will be a culture of love...*SEE Culture.* For when we feel out of balance or "out of whack," we become disconnected from higher consciousness. Following this simple logic, to find balance in one's life is essential to living in love. SEE Culture promotes and supports a healthy balance in society; this in turn increases the likelihood that we as individuals living in that society will find the balance we need to achieve higher consciousness. Think of it in terms of "you are what you eat," or, as discussed earlier, being products of our environment—mind, body, and spirit.

SEE Balance

I am not the first to propose that the path to higher consciousness and love comes down to balance. Recognizing that love identifies with all and takes sides with none, to be completely balanced means to exist between the innumerable dichotomies with which we otherwise might wrestle. In mathematical or geometric terms, this means returning to the origin, the place of infinite possibility:

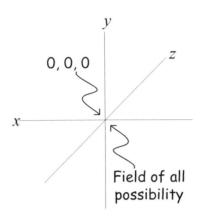

Let us use SEE VISUAL AID to understand the nature of being present in this **field of all possibility**. Start by imagining yourself occupying an infinitely small point at the origin of the universe. Three interesting observations can be made. First, since you are not in the universe of form, practically speaking, but can see in all directions from your vantage point, you have a complete, balanced, and unbiased view of the cosmos. You are the ultimate observer. Second, you have an equal opportunity to head out into the universe in any direction; no axis or direction appears more or less burdensome to you; travelling along all possible trajectories or to any equidistant points in the universe would require the exact same expenditure of time and energy. Third, whether the universe is expanding or contracting is irrelevant, since your position at its absolute origin (0, 0, 0) means universal forces of expansion or contraction cancel each other out and your position is completely secure. You are not subject to the conditions which apply elsewhere in the universe. Mathematically speaking, zero multiplied or divided by any other number is still zero. Zero can only change its nature if it is added to or subtracted from, but as zero it exists unconditionally in the field of all possibility.

You have likely heard people talk about being centred, feeling grounded, standing on solid ground, or finding their footing in life. It is fair to say that these expressions capture the essence of being balanced. Like any high-rise structure, the higher one hopes to reach, the stronger the foundation one must build upon. Think of sprinters who take their marks by firmly planting their feet in a pair of solid starting blocks. The feeling of confidence that comes from knowing you're starting off on solid footing also lends to the idea that tomorrow is another day. After all, if you made it this far, you know the starting blocks will still be there waiting for you tomorrow. This is very liberating, because it frees you from ego attachment to the outcome of the race. You may win or you may lose, but no matter what the outcome, you can always return to where you are right now, in this moment: feet firmly planted, balanced, at the origin, in the field of infinite possibility. So-called "bad things" will happen. Failure, like death, is just another part of life. Walking along the path of life takes balance; sometimes you will be tripped up and fall down. So what do you do? You pick yourself up, brush yourself off, regain your balance and your footing, and continue along the journey. There's no mysticism or ancient secret to it; it's pretty much just common sense. The young of all species in nature learning to walk, climb, swim, swing, or fly practice it. If they falter, they use the opportunity to learn and grow from the experience. Failure is just another life lesson: if you can see it and feel it as unconditional love, you will be empowered by all your experiences, both the "good" and the "bad," and in all aspects of your being: mind, body, and spirit.

Mind, Body, Spirit

SEE BALANCE

The Rewards

Now what? We have followed an argument from the big-picture concept of culture, through its evolution, and its implications in terms of human nature, the narrative story arc of human societies—conflict and consumption—down to the level of individual balance. Has all this simply been an inverted way to explain the classic approach to higher consciousness (that is, beginning with the individual and moving outward to the big picture)? Not at all. Culture is behind everything. It is indivisible from that which we define as human nature at any given point in time, including what we might call happiness and development, on both the personal and societal level.

SEE Growth in Personal & Societal Happiness & Development

A SEE Culture that promotes balance among its citizens, and advances the evolution of the species toward higher consciousness influences not only the personal growth of individuals and society as a whole, but the long-term integrity of community, institutions, traditions, and enterprises.

  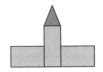

SEE Long-term Integrity in Community, Institutions, Government & Industry

The rewards of a balanced, SEE Culture reach into every aspect of human existence, and, far from being boring, this new human experience represents a field of infinite possibility. Enlightened individuals have spoken for millennia about the infinite potential that becomes available to an individual when he or she "steps through the gate." Now imagine the opportunities that become available when whole communities, institutions, enterprises, governments, societies, or the planet as a whole awaken to infinite potential. Impossible you say? Perhaps, but what makes more sense: believing it's impossible, thereby perpetuating a culture whose legacy is conflict, consumption, and human suffering, or taking a chance that it just might be possible and embracing a culture that promotes balance and higher consciousness? What's the worst that could happen by taking a chance—and taking action—on humanity's infinite potential?

Call to Action

SEE Culture is not a pipe dream. Mainstream media and business are beginning to catch on to the concepts of balance and human beings' desire to live happier, fuller, more meaningful lives. What many artists, musicians, writers, filmmakers, restaurateurs, and other purveyors of culture have discovered is that when you get that balance just right, you open a gate to higher consciousness, to unconditional love. A far cry from being desirable or addictive, a product, service, or work of culture that connects with people on the level of love is *irresistible*. It's impossible to fake this connection and attempts to short-change the process often miss the mark and fail miserably. There is a long history of traditions dating back thousands of years and spanning continents that have produced tried, tested, and true processes for achieving exactly the kind of balance between entertainment and enrichment that is needed. We will look more closely at the process in Volume two. In the meantime, if you want the inside scoop, and to become an active contributor and benefactor of a new SEE Culture, visit www.attlas.org.

SEE Progress

❶ (a) Economics   (b) SEEconomics

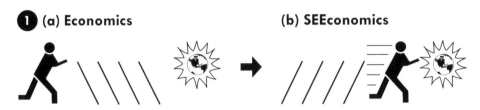

Backward, limiting materialism progresses via enlightened, empowering value systems.

❷ (a) Democracy   (b) SEE Democracy

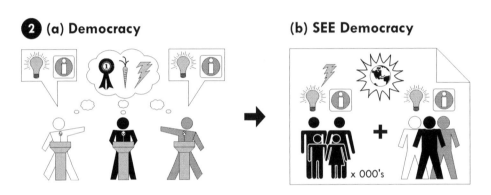

Partisan power struggles usurped by the people's collaborative collective consciousness.

❸ (a) Conflict/Consumer Culture   (b) SEE Culture

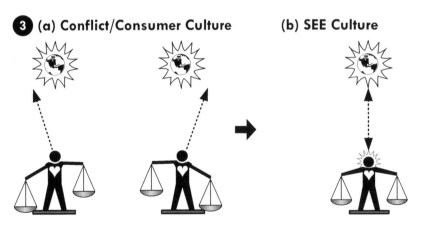

Extremism and misalignment give way to balance and connection to higher consciousness.

CHAPTER FIVE
SEE PROGRESS

So What?

While enrolled in Wilfrid Laurier University's MBA program, a simple concept was embedded in my consciousness: "So what?" It was a question hammered in and hammered home by every professor. The notion is this: an idea, strategy, discourse, or course of action may be all well and good, but what practical, meaningful significance (and/or consequence) will it have in the real world, in the short and the long term? My professors asked this question within the context of business (for profit and non-profit), but I saw it applying to all forms of human enterprise—economic, governmental, cultural, even personal. This notion truly began to crystallize for me partway through my master's degree, when I first conceived of SEEconomics. It was early 2002, and while the world was trying to come to terms with the events of 9/11 in the usual way (reacting to aggression, hatred, and fear with fear, anger, and aggression—renewing the cycle of violence) I was asking "so what?" What could I do to break that cycle? I wrote my thesis on SEEconomics and conceived the Attlas Project as a business plan—*a neo-enterprise for the 21st century*. It would be an enterprise that stood as a triad, linking for-profit, not-for-profit, and public spheres. It would apply change theory and SEE VISUAL AID (which at that time was called Strategic Communications) to work with all three to make SEEconomics a reality. Suffice it to say that at the time and in the years since, policies in Ottawa and Washington (not to mention attitudes on Wall Street and Bay Street) produced little interest and left me with little hope, apart from the moral support of those who knew me and my efforts personally.

They say nothing lasts forever, every dog has his day, and there's nothing more powerful than an idea whose time has come. There were some dramatic changes in the world in 2008. We saw a few micro-opportunities seized by investment gurus, banking executives, and OPEC balloon into a plethora of macro-effects on a global scale whose full force and consequences have yet to be experienced. We also saw the micro-opportunities seized by the likes of Rosa Parks, Martin Luther King Jr., Jesse Jackson, and Oprah Winfrey—and countless other unnamed and unsung social leaders—explode in the macro-effect of the election of Barack Obama. But make no mistake: Mr. Obama's ethnicity and heritage (like everyone's) is just the seed of his person. It was the power of his message—hope and change—which broke new ground once hardened by entrenched political ideologies to kindle and capture the imagination of a people. These are the people who now wait—along with the rest of the world—and watch Mr. Obama in full bloom, to see how he manages the storm of the global recession, and what fruit his presidency will bear. It should come as no surprise, then, that twenty years since drawing my first VISUAL AID and seven years since conceiving of SEEconomics and the Attlas Project, I would feel that the time for people to *SEE the world in a new light* was finally here, now. No matter who you are, what hand you've been dealt, or what hats you wear—politician, business leader, activist, artist, consumer, voter, and so forth—the time has come to SEE the world and your place in it in a new light: namely, your absolute potential to be an agent of positive change and personal growth. Not only in your own life for your own sake, but for the sake of the planet and all of humankind.

What can *I* do? For starters, I took the "I" and the apostrophe (signifying possession) out of "Attila's Project." The Attlas Project is not *my* project, it is *our* project. It is *your* project, should you take the next step.

What's Next?

Thus far, we have taken a more or less exclusively secular look at the world. We began in the introduction by looking at ways to create change on a macro, system-wide level just by making minor—but intentional—upgrades to the system itself. We followed that with a handful of easy-to-follow instructions for upgrading several systems of humankind—a set of micro-opportunities that, if seized today, will lead to positive macro-effects in the future. I believe I have made an internally consistent and valid argument for each upgrade to human civilization proposed in Volume one, on a more-or-less secular line of argumentation. I intentionally kept faith-based, dogmatic, and so-called New Age arguments to an absolute minimum, appealing instead to the rational, scientific, bottom-line-oriented mind in all of us for whom SEEing is believing. Volume one is rooted in pure logic, a basic appreciation for human rights, and the universal intention of all beings to exist, persist, survive, and thrive, along with their environment. For human beings, this happens to encapsulate the whole planet and all its systems. Based on this approach alone, there should be enough information and impetus here for all of us—no matter what we may or may not believe spiritually—to start acting on the Attlas Project.

Taking on the Weight of the World

SEEing a brighter potential future is one thing; making it a reality always seems to be what trips up the best of our visions and intentions. It's easy to blame our inability to achieve a more "perfect" society on the fact that we human beings simply don't like change, but as discussed in the introduction, it's more about what *kind* of change we face.

An Example of *Intention* at Work in a Cause and Effect Change Process

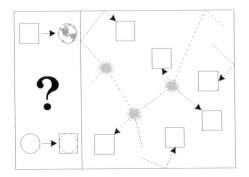

Define the Crisis and/or *Opportunity*.
A square peg won't "work" given a round hole; so an entrenched system of square pegs, evolved over many generations (and acting / interacting accordingly), certainly won't "work" in a world that is defined by round holes. Luckily, every square has an inherent *potential for roundness* inside.

Create and Communicate an *Intention*.
Formulate and introduce (envision and inspire; design and install) *the intention for roundness* into the established system of square pegs.

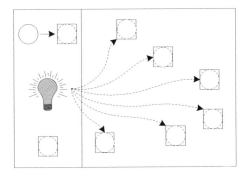

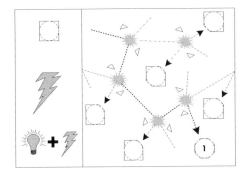

Act (and Interact) with Intention.
The system, with the intention of roundness installed, functions as usual producing small incremental changes to participants with every action / interaction. The change process is accelerated by proactive participants focused on *their intention*—and *their potential*—for roundness (1).

Wait and Watch the *Transformation*.
Many generations of intentional actions and interactions, each having just a small incremental effect on participants, will over time produce the intended transformation; first, on an individual basis (1); then system wide: a system of square pegs *transformed* for a world full of round holes.

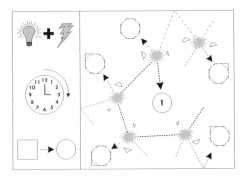

I've made a point of illustrating how the Attlas Project does not propose a throw-the-baby-out-with-the-bathwater approach to progress. As someone who has explored all manner of mythology, religion, spirituality, scientific theory, and metaphysics, especially their visions for the future—idyllic, apocalyptic, and post-apocalyptic combos of all kinds—I found two recurring constants. First, all these paradigms of thought purport to illuminate the path by which humankind will achieve a higher state of being. Second, they all seem to demand a sacrifice of one fundamental aspect of human nature or another. Like it or not, we live in a world that asks the question, "So what?" It's all well and good for the spiritual, religious, and self-righteous faithful of all kinds to preach poverty, abstinence, obedience, and even violence, but what practical, meaningful significance (and/or consequence) do their teachings and actions have in the real world, for the whole world (near and long term)? My intention in Volume one of *the Attlas Project* was to give you—the reader; the world—a *doable* vision for progress that builds upon the systems we know and live with every day. It's a vision for embracing the evolution of our species and progressing from where we are at today.

As it happens I do believe in God (spirit, higher consciousness, etc.), that a much better world is intended for humankind, and that it awaits us over the horizon. The journey of a thousand miles begins, they say, with a single step, and history and biology teach us that as a species we are more likely to take baby steps than some giant leap of faith imposed dogmatically by a few upon the rest. Unless, of course, crisis calls for revolutionary change, as so many dire prophecies of the future predict. Either way, there's nothing to fear. In mythology, Atlas holds up the pillars of earth and heaven. Take a moment to review the VISUAL AIDs in this book. You will SEE it all come together: when you **SEE the world in a new light,** it follows you can then...

SEE THE LIGHT OF THE WORLD

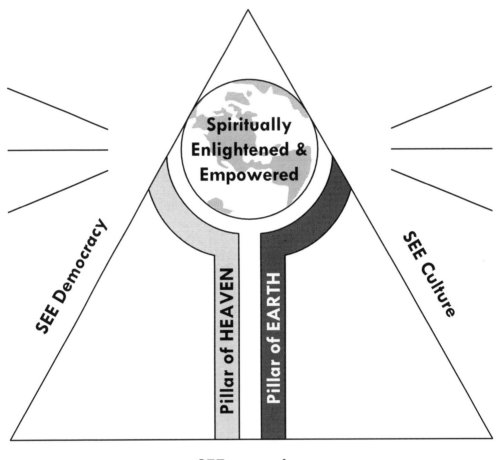

Spiritually Enlightened & Empowered

SEE Democracy

SEE Culture

Pillar of HEAVEN

Pillar of EARTH

SEEconomics

THE ATTLAS PROJECT

VOLUME TWO

E P I L O G U E
SEE A PREVIEW OF
VOLUME TWO

SEE a New Definition: Spiritually Enlightened and Empowered

In Volume one of *the Attlas Project*, "SEE" stood for Strategize, Engage, Execute as in SEE VISUAL AID, Social, Environmental Economics, or SEEconomics, Society Engaged Electronic Democracy (SEE Democracy), and Society Enriching and Entertaining Culture—SEE Culture. It is safe to say that Volume one took a mostly secular approach, focusing on the "pillar of earth". In Volume two we will SEE (Strategize, Engage, Execute) the world beyond the world of form, to SEE the pillars of heaven and earth, the support they lend and the gate they create for us. So "SEE" takes on one last definition—its ultimate meaning: **Spiritually Enlightened and Empowered,** as in **SEE Planet.**

The Origins of SEE VISUAL AID

Like all spiritual journeys, the path that brought me to this point in my life has been personal, and holds great meaning for me. Since SEE VISUAL AID is so fundamental to the Attlas Project, I feel it's important to share a history of events that I believe point to some greater force at work behind its conception. Telling this story is also an opportunity for me to make a deeper connection with you the reader in contrast to the more clinical, matter-of-fact approach I took in Volume one.

My father was born and raised in Hungary, where he studied to become a designer. He and my mother defected to Austria in 1966, where they lived the high life in Vienna (where my father had an excellent job as an up-and-coming designer) until the Czechoslovakian Revolution in 1968. The Austrian authorities gathered up all the immigrants from Soviet-Bloc countries and my parents were told which countries to which they could apply to emigrate, including Sweden and Australia. My mother had relatives living in the United States; her grandparents lived in South Bend, Indiana, having fled to the U.S. during the 1956 Hungarian Revolution. During the application process, however, my father disclosed his military service (military duty was mandatory in Hungary at the time and as a stout, athletic individual my father had served his time as a paratrooper) and it was made clear to him that if they wanted to become U.S. citizens, he would have to go fight in Vietnam. Now, I don't have to tell you this did not go over well with the young couple. In the words of my mother, "We did not spend the better part of our lives escaping the Communists in Europe to go fight the Communists in Asia!" In December 1968, the Liberal government of Pierre Trudeau sent word to Austria that Canada's doors were open, and ten days later, my parents arrived in Montreal, Quebec: tired, hungry, and—unable to speak English or French—truly strangers in a strange land.

Fortune smiled on them again, this time because of a very bold, boisterous, and bombastic Hungarian fellow whom I would know as Kovács. He was a resident of Windsor, Ontario, a fairly prominent member of a vibrant Hungarian community in the area, and fairly well-connected to boot. He helped my father enrol in Chrysler University for Engineering and got him a job on the assembly line on the night shift, putting the massive chrome bumpers on the cars that were still the rage in the late sixties.

During this time, the Detroit race riots were taking place and my parents would sit on the Canadian side of the Detroit River and watch the city burning in the night. Two years after fleeing their homeland to escape the perils of Communism, they went from living free and well-off lives in Austria, frequenting the opera house and sitting by its picturesque outdoor cafes, to sitting on the banks of a river in a foreign land watching an entire city ablaze in hatred. This was not exactly what they had in mind when they left Hungary in the first place, and certainly went against every concept they had about the West—their hopes and dreams for a better life in a country where freedom, peace, and justice prevailed seemed to be going up in smoke before their eyes.

If that wasn't enough to shake their confidence, when the union workers on the midnight shift found out my father was studying by day to become a "white-collar traitor to the blue collar man," he was handed a pink slip. His hopes of getting his engineering degree at Chrysler University evaporated (although he would eventually get an industrial engineering degree from York University some years later). With only his degree in fashion design in hand, he and my mother moved to Toronto, where the bulk of the needle trade was in Canada. My father went knocking on doors on Spadina Avenue and was able to find work in the fashion industry, eventually landing a job as assistant designer. When my brother was born in 1970, in the middle of the night, my father did the traditional thing: he went out into the streets handing out cigars. The only people he found at that time of night were homeless people, so he gave them cigars. They in turn brought out the booze, and together they all went into an all-night restaurant, and that's how my father celebrated the birth of his first son. Needless to say, he was late for work the following morning, and his boss was not impressed, not even by the cigar my father had saved for him. "Who cares about your son?" he said to my dad. Well, suffice it to say that my father had some choice remarks in return, and was fired that day. The story became a popular bit of gossip in the fashion district, however, and when it reached the ears of the owner of Best Outerwear, my father received a phone call from Bernie Goldberger, the owner, who knew my father only by name and reputation as a former up-and-coming designer in Austria. With a fairly good job at Bernie's, my dad and mum finally put down roots, and in 1973, I became the newest member of the family. I would spend my first decade living in Toronto and one of its suburbs, Thornhill.

Some years later, my family and I found ourselves living in Guelph, Ontario, where my father became director of manufacturing for Rennie Inc., a family-owned shirt manufacturing business of some 500 employees. A few years later, I would find myself in my first job, working as a part-time salesclerk at K-Mart. When I turned 13, my older brother and I purchased our first real computer—an IBM XT clone—and it was around that time that I became my father's personal secretary. He would convey his memos and letters to me at night which I would help him compose, edit, and print on the computer. Remember, this was a brilliant man whose areas of expertise were design and engineering. We would joke in my family that the only thing worse than my dad's English was his Hungarian! Truly, language was never my father's strong suit, and he never came close to mastering English. And yet, when asked about the secret to his successful management style, his answer was always the same: "Talk to the people."

By 1988, the Progressive Conservative government of Brian Mulroney had negotiated a major free-trade agreement with the United States (which would eventually form the foundations of NAFTA—the North American Free Trade Agreement). The effects of free trade were felt throughout the manufacturing sector in Canada, but its impact on the needle trade was nothing short of devastating. I actually worked full-time in the factory during the summer, and saw first hand my father's efforts to build a defence against losing work to offshore suppliers of cheaper (now duty-free) imports. Since my father not only ran the plant but also designed all the shirts, he could see the big picture from beginning to end, and looked to technology for a way to automate, streamline, and inject a new level of efficiency into an otherwise labour-intensive process. He designed a workflow automation plan for the plant that incorporated a French-made CAD / robotic cutting system (by Lectra Systems) and a separate inventory management system. This was a good start, but implementing these technologies was going to be a challenge in a factory whose employees were mostly immigrant women with English and computer skills at the same level or lower than my father's.

By this time my father and I had developed a fairly efficient way of working together when it came to preparing communiqués for the factory. I was onto my second computer, which had a colour screen running Windows 3.1. What would change my life, believe it or not, was a piece of software I picked up in a bargain bin at a computer show in Toronto. The software was called *Visio*, an object-oriented program for technical drawing. Its user interface was based on the concept of green drafting stencils, the kind you'd typically find at a stationary store, useful for drawing geometric shapes and other symbols to exacting standards. This simple CAD program came chock-full of these stencils, which allowed you to simply drag and drop shapes onto the page where you could resize, colour, label, and manipulate them in ways that should be familiar to anyone who has ever worked with computer graphics of any kind. While I had no need of preparing circuit board layouts or schematic diagrams, I found this simple drawing tool indispensible when it came to many things, including helping my mother rearrange furniture in the house, creating diagrams for school projects, and, of course, helping my father in his major work project.

Speaking of rearranging furniture, if you have ever done it in the traditional way, you know that it can be back-breaking work. It can also be demoralizing and discouraging if, after you've rearranged everything, it just doesn't work. Now forget about a few hundred square feet and imagine having to deal with hundreds of thousands of square feet, and you get a sense of what it means to rework the floor plan of a factory. That is exactly what we did, my dad and I. Using the floor plan layout stencils in Visio, I was able to take dimensions provided to me by my father for everything from plant size and pillar locations to work tables, sewing stations, and even carts and conveyor belts. Using the computer, we could move, rotate, arrange and rearrange any and all elements found in the factory infinitely—and believe me, it sometimes felt like it would never end. We did eventually strike upon a configuration that worked, but this was only the beginning.

As we were rearranging the plant in preparation for the technology implementation, my father was rearranging his mind (and calming his nerves) trying to wrap his head around how that technology worked. He was born in 1939, after all. He hadn't even owned a calculator until sometime after I was born. It didn't help that a good deal of the documentation for the CAD system he alone would be using was in French. Being more computer-literate and knowing a bit more French meant I translated as best I could, but this was a proprietary, industrial-grade computer system unlike any I had ever used before, so my father did most of the learning on his own. When the plant finally took delivery of the Lectra system, he spent hours working hands-on with it. All his cardboard patterns needed to be digitized and loaded into the computer where the individual pieces that made up multiple sizes of shirt could be arranged to align properly with fabric patterns and minimize waste. By now, he had plenty of time learning the basics of working with CAD with all the work we did with Visio, so once he got his hands on the proprietary Lectra system, he was well on his way to mastering the technology.

When it finally came to implementing my father's work-flow system in the factory, he turned once again to me to help him write the memos and guides that could quickly and effectively communicate the new procedures workers would need to follow. There was no point writing a lot of words to accomplish this: many of the supervisors who needed to be trained and who in turn would train others were immigrants, too. The answer was to show and tell. My father would never leave the fate of anyone's knowledge and self-confidence in the hands of a memo; he would do the telling himself, while I would prepare for him simple VISUAL AIDs that served as tools and handy references for the future. In the end, the implementation and transition to the new system went relatively smoothly, and for a number of years, the company would not only survive NAFTA, it would thrive and grow.

EPILOGUE

As for myself and SEE VISUAL AID, I would use it as a tool throughout my life: in university; teaching English in Japan; working for an internet company and its strategic partner, IBM, during the dot-com era; in my consulting business; and most importantly, in understanding and rearranging the flow of my life—where I was at any given moment, what events had led up to that point, and what paths might lead me to where I needed to go. It was shortly after I turned thirty that I began to SEE *everything* in terms of shapes and patterns: not just the flow of cause and effect, but the intention behind it, including my life and my place in the world. There were no more accidents. Events literally began falling into place, even so-called tragedies. I had always had a deep intuitive knowing about who I was, and what I was meant to do in my life, but this inner feeling didn't always seem to mesh with what was happening in my life—nor with the expectations and demands of others. I think we can all relate to the anxiety that comes from self-doubt and asking questions like, "What if my intuition and passion for living a life of purpose is *wrong*?" And, "What if everyone around me is right and I'm just living a pipe dream?" Or, worse, "Am I abnormal?" I don't ask questions like that anymore, not since I began to SEE the world and my place in it as a divine gift—warts and all—each and every person and event perfectly aligned with the intention of spirit. In fact, it was after losing a client and getting into a car accident that I was inspired to write this book—in perfect timing with Barack Obama's election and the global financial crisis. There are no accidents. When you can SEE the world in that light, you can SEE the light of the world: there is no "good" and "bad," "heaven" and "earth." Heaven is the earth. It *is* possible to SEE.

SEEing is Believing

In Volume one, we saw the power of SEE VISUAL AID as a system for observing, analyzing, re-thinking, and then re-constructing the world to create win-win-win scenarios. As a tool for solving problems, SEE VISUAL AID does appear to have an edge over any other single form of discourse, because it draws on any and all discourses as necessary without being bound by the limits of any one of them. For instance, you will recall that while SEE VISUAL AID is clearly logical, it is not bound by the general linearity of logic, which cannot handle too many variables at once (at least, not without the aid of a supercomputer). Einstein said "Imagination is more important than knowledge," and SEE VISUAL AID definitely falls into the space of imagination—taken literally, it is an imaging system, a way for us to make sense of our world. While I won't reproduce it here, it is a worthwhile exercise to visit Wikipedia and read the excerpt there about imagination (http://en.wikipedia.org/wiki/Imagination). That is all well and good—imagination helps us make sense of our world—but what about that which is *beyond* our world? What about those anomalies, beliefs, etc., that are unseen and unproven (scientifically unsolved)? How far can we stretch the limits of SEE VISUAL AID's capabilities? Can it be applied, for example, in the highly personal space of spiritual belief and the even more contentious space of religious dogma?

Certainly in the West—and in Roman Catholicism and Christianity in general—there has been no shortage of individuals throughout history who have used their imagination to embellish the words of scriptures and prophets. From the ceiling of the Sistine Chapel to Dante's *Inferno* to the *Angels in America* television series, people have imagined what events from the Bible may have looked like, what life after death *might be like,* and how other beliefs they have *might work.* In some cases, Church leaders commissioned these imaginations (the art in the Sistine Chapel, for instance), in other cases, religious leaders—and not just in the West—have railed against imaginations of the sacred as "blasphemous". Salman Rushdie was famously scorned, threatened, and even faced religious edict (*fatwā*) by some fundamentalist Muslims and their leaders for his novel, *The Satanic Verses.* In addition, Islam condemns any graphic depiction of the prophet Mohammad as heretical. The attempt by those in power to control visions of faith is ironic; whether religious officials like it or not, no one among the faithful is able to believe without imagination. What we understand as having faith lies in the realm beyond the senses. If you think about concepts like heaven and hell, what can you do other than visualize what they might be like? To believe in anything is to see it in your mind's eye, to imagine what the unseen world of spirit is really like.

It should come as no surprise that no two people's imaginations (or scriptural descriptions) of any aspect of religion is identical. This poses a bit of a problem, doesn't it? Well, yes and no. Consider this: if *any* aspect of the human condition is about "the big picture," surely religion is it, so certain details are pretty much irrelevant. Whether heaven is a bunch of clouds in the sky or a lush garden of infinite majesty, and the exact number of vestal virgins awaiting a Muslim martyr, are more or less irrelevant compared to the general themes and functions of faith as a whole (i.e., heaven is a nice place to spend eternity; any number of vestal virgins is probably incentive enough for angry, impoverished youth living in Gaza to be recruited as suicide bombers). Of course, making this rational argument presents the believer with a slippery slope—when do appropriate imaginations cross the line into blasphemy? After all, when one does a bird's-eye survey of the world's religions, one sees tremendous overlap in many beliefs and traditions, and yet at times it strikes me as madness the details of religious belief for which people are willing to kill and die. Even setting aside the tensions between major world religions, you need look no further than the bad blood that can exist between sects of the *same* religious traditions—Protestants and Catholics (both Christian); Shiites and Sunnis (both Muslim). So faith is a big-picture subject, supposedly scientifically unsolvable, and riddled with details—some open to imagination and interpretation that don't really matter in the grand scheme of things, and others that appear to be of direct significance to religious leaders and believers and have been at the root of countless religious schisms.

I would absolutely contend that VISUAL AID can help people SEE (think about, engage others about, and act upon) their spiritual and religious beliefs.

SEE VISUAL AID and Lao Tzu's Wisdom Revealed

Have you ever heard the Taoist expression, "it's the space between the bars that holds of the tiger?" If so, have you ever thought about it? I have heard many spiritual gurus make reference to this quotation without actually providing an explanation as to what Lao Tzu might have meant by it. At best, they present it in the context of some existential philosophy; at worst, it's seen as just another in a series of arcane ramblings by an ancient Chinese master. Aligning our thinking back with Volume one of this book, is it possible to act on the wisdom of that quotation? Can we SEE (Strategize, Engage, Execute) what Lao Tzu meant by it? Let's use a VISUAL AID and SEE how far we get.

Here is a tiger behind some bars. Now, any pragmatist will tell you that it is, in fact, the bars that hold the tiger and not the empty space between them. After all, that is simply the nature of a tiger, and the nature of metal bars. One could argue that the space between the bars is defined by the distance the bars are spaced, and therefore, too narrow a space between the bars is, in fact, what prevents the tiger from escaping. This is more a clever play on words and logic, however, than a revelation of profound spiritual wisdom. What is needed here is an entirely different perspective on the question. In other words, we need to SEE it differently.

   Now what holds the tiger? Here we see the same scene from a different point of view—that of the tiger. What's more, for all intents and purposes, it is the most important point of view. After all, it's the tiger that's being held, not us. How are we to know what's holding back the tiger unless we climb under his skin, get behind his eyes, and look at the situation from his point of view? Again, speaking purely pragmatically, as a tiger, could we see through iron bars? Of course not: our view is made possible by virtue of the space between the bars. And, if—as a tiger—we are looking through the spaces between bars, in all likelihood we are in a zoo, circus, or some other man-made cage. What we are likely to see, then, are people—the keeper, parents, children—in other words, our human *captors*. In reality, iron bars hold nothing without the intent of captors to hold something behind them—in this case a tiger—*us*. When seen from the captive tiger's perspective, the space between the bars reveals what truly holds us captive: *our captors*. Did they not exist there would be no bars. Captors are what we tigers see and "Were it not for my captors, I would be free" is what we tigers believe. It is in our nature as tigers to believe what we see, and if what we see are captors, then what we believe is that we are captive—we are *victims* of captivity, as it were.

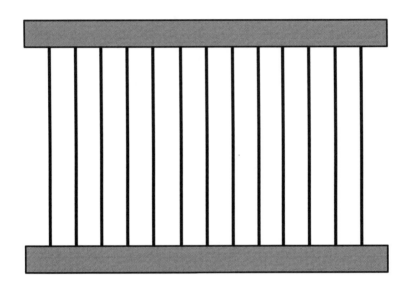

Now what holds the tiger? Surely the circus or the zoo must close sometime. Now what do we, the tiger, see in the space between the bars? Nothing: in fact, there is never actually anything in the space between the bars other than what we tigers choose to believe there is, based on what we see. Nothing is really holding us tigers back. As we have seen, however, it is the nature of the tiger to see himself as captive, a victim, and believe that which he sees. It is therefore his nature as a victim that holds him back, nothing more. Lao Tzu asks: why be a tiger, then, and be held by nothing but your own nature as a victim? Why not choose to be the opposite of a tiger and no longer be held by the space between the bars. Why not become *a dragon* instead?

Most people will be aware of the yin and yang symbol of the Tao. The whole of the universe exists in the eternal interplay of the positive and negative (black and white, unseen and seen, spiritual and corporeal, etc.) halves of reality, each of which contains the potential for its opposite within itself. The Shaolin way of looking at the yin and yang is the dragon and the tiger. The phrase *Crouching Tiger, Hidden Dragon* is not just the title of an award-winning film by Ang Lee, it is a description of the Tao and the relationship between the personification of

yin—or positive energy—as the magical dragon, and yang—or negative energy—as the corporeal tiger. The nature of the tiger is to see his physical limitations and constraints and believe that he is subject to those limitations and constraints (which he is, since that is his nature, as we have seen). Were he able to realize that he has the potential to be a dragon, however, he would awaken to his own unlimited potential—and then nothing in the subjective world of form could hold him. In Chinese tradition, the dragon is a creature of pure objective potentiality that can move freely between the worlds of form and formlessness. As a dragon, one could easily slip through the space between the bars. What holds back the tiger cannot hold back the dragon. That is Lao Tzu's message to us: if you are a tiger held back by your nature that believes you exist only in the world of physical form—and can therefore be held—remember your dragon potential, and be held back by nothing.

This is Lao Tzu's wisdom: abandon your negativity, your victim mentality, and your belief in limits. Stop blaming everyone and everything around you for holding you back, because, in truth, nothing is holding you back except your belief that your freedom is subject to your circumstances. Search within yourself and you will find the "hidden dragon"—your positive nature, your heavenly power, your spirit, which can move freely between the worlds of form and formlessness—a being without limits. *Be a dragon.*

Or, if you can't relate to this Asian mythological symbol (i.e., you see dragons as dangerous, scary, or evil) then turn instead to the Western mythological tradition of Atlas, who upholds the pillars of heaven *and* earth, the seen and unseen. With these two pillars in place, you not only have an arch—one of the simplest, yet most stable architectural forms—upon which to raise your world, you create a gate—a space between the pillars, as it were—that you can freely pass through at will: your own personal gateway to SEE the unseen and know, first-hand, the "scientifically unknowable".

APPENDIX
VISUAL SUMMARY

SEE THE WORLD IN A NEW LIGHT

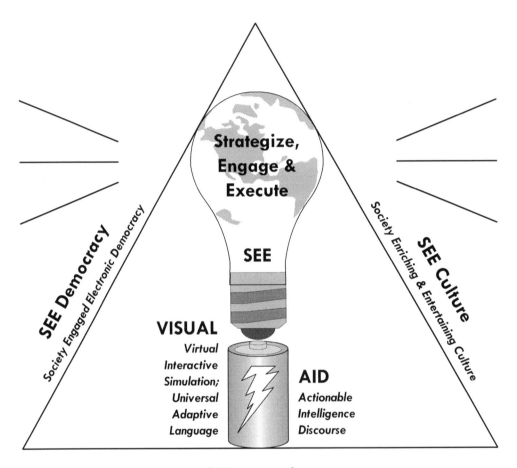

Strategize, Engage & Execute

SEE

SEE Democracy
Society Engaged Electronic Democracy

SEE Culture
Society Enriching & Entertaining Culture

VISUAL
Virtual
Interactive
Simulation;
Universal
Adaptive
Language

AID
Actionable
Intelligence
Discourse

SEEconomics
Social & Environmental Economics

THE ATTLAS PROJECT

VOLUME ONE

SEE VISUAL AID

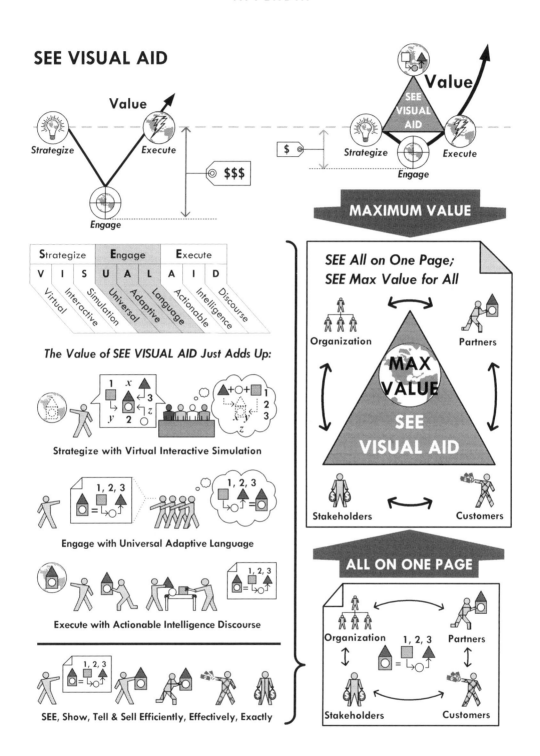

The Value of SEE VISUAL AID Just Adds Up:

Strategize with Virtual Interactive Simulation

Engage with Universal Adaptive Language

Execute with Actionable Intelligence Discourse

SEE, Show, Tell & Sell Efficiently, Effectively, Exactly

SEE All on One Page;
SEE Max Value for All

Social Environmental Economics

START with *Economics as we know it:*

Forces of Social, Environmental & Economic
Progress "Railroaded" by *Business As Usual*

NEXT, *SEE* **a New Direction for Business:**

1 Vehicle - *SEE Valuation*

2 Platform - *SEE Commerce*

3 Passengers - *SEE Stakeholder Value*

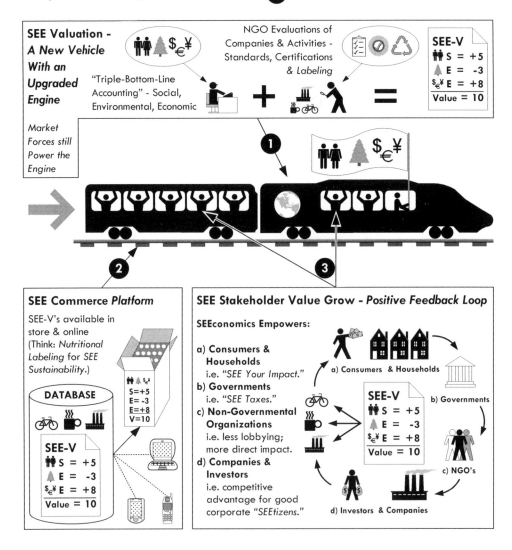

SEE Valuation -
A New Vehicle
With an
Upgraded
Engine

"Triple-Bottom-Line Accounting" - Social, Environmental, Economic

NGO Evaluations of Companies & Activities - Standards, Certifications & Labeling

SEE-V
S = +5
E = -3
E = +8
Value = 10

Market Forces still Power the Engine

SEE Commerce *Platform*

SEE-V's available in store & online (Think: *Nutritional Labeling for SEE Sustainability.*)

DATABASE

SEE-V
S = +5
E = -3
E = +8
Value = 10

S=+5
E= -3
E=+8
V=10

SEE Stakeholder Value Grow - *Positive Feedback Loop*

SEEconomics Empowers:

a) **Consumers &**
Households
i.e. *"SEE Your Impact."*

b) **Governments**
i.e. *"SEE Taxes."*

c) **Non-Governmental**
Organizations
i.e. less lobbying; more direct impact.

d) **Companies &**
Investors
i.e. competitive advantage for good corporate *"SEEtizens."*

a) Consumers & Households

SEE-V
S = +5
E = -3
E = +8
Value = 10

b) Governments

c) NGO's

d) Investors & Companies

Society Engaged Electronic Democracy

THE KEY: *WikiPolicy* – REAL Power in REAL-TIME, via Wiki-Technology Similar to *Wikipedia*.

Society Enriching & Entertaining Culture

SEE Growth in Personal & Societal Happiness & Development

Art

Books

Theatre

Film

Mind, Body, Spirit

Music

Food & Drink

Crafts & Antiquities

SEE BALANCE

Television

I.T. & Internet

Shopping

Sports & Exercise

Games

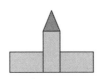

SEE Long-term Integrity in Community, Institutions, Government & Industry

SEE Progress

❶ (a) Economics   (b) SEEconomics

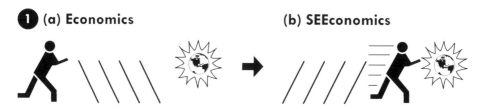

Backward, limiting materialism progresses via enlightened, empowering value systems.

❷ (a) Democracy   (b) SEE Democracy

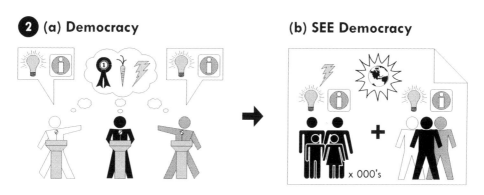

Partisan power struggles usurped by the people's collaborative collective consciousness.

❸ (a) Conflict/Consumer Culture   (b) SEE Culture

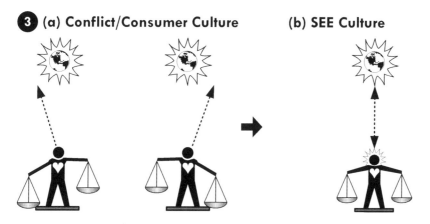

Extremism and misalignment give way to balance and connection to higher consciousness.

SEE THE LIGHT
OF THE WORLD

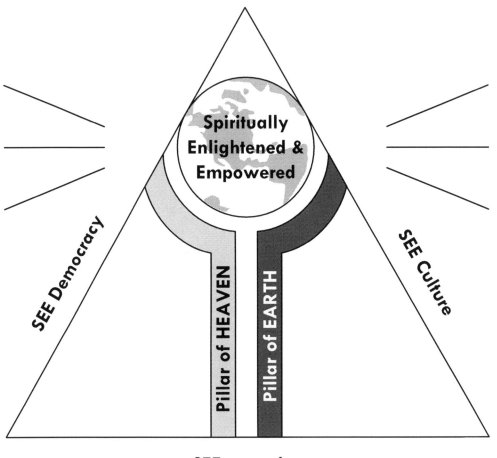

Spiritually Enlightened & Empowered

SEE Democracy

Pillar of HEAVEN

Pillar of EARTH

SEE Culture

SEEconomics

THE ATTLAS PROJECT

VOLUME TWO

30212864R00104

Made in the USA
Charleston, SC
09 June 2014